2022
Year in Review

All Roads Lead to Ukraine

David B. Collum

David B. Collum
Betty R. Miller Professor of Chemistry and Chemical Biology
Cornell University
Email: dbc6@cornell.edu
Twitter: @DavidBCollum

Copyediting and layout by Jeremy Irwin
Edited by Robert Moriarty

Library of Congress Cataloging-in-Publication Data has been applied for.

ISBN: 979-8-386-21439-5

FOREWORD BY THE EDITOR

More years ago than I prefer to count, a chemistry professor from Cornell University sent an unsolicited piece of work to me, in the hope that Barb and I would post it on our website at 321gold.com.

We read it. We laughed a lot at how outrageously the writer wrote. We posted it under an assumed name. The author wasn't sure what its reception might be, so requested his real name not be used.

That was 2008. The next year the same writer did another piece commenting on all the insanity of 2009, now simply calling it 2009 Year in Review. Since then, as revealed by David B. Collum, his yearly review has become one of the most read commentaries on the web.

It's probably not because so many people agree with every unconventional thought out of David's mouth. If you can't find something in any one of the reviews that offends you, he has done a poor job indeed. You can't possibly agree with every comment, but he speaks simply and directly. In a world seemingly filled with idiots sounding as if they have a mouth full of marbles, David Collum is nothing short of remarkable.

He is never boring. I wish I could say the same.

I look forward each December to the appearance of another Year in Review on the web. But it occurred to me that they would make great books; readers could then easily go back and reread his thoughts from years before. So I twisted David's arm and here we are in print.

Robert Moriarty
February 2023

CONTENTS

PART ONE

(continued)

CONTENTS *(continued)*

PART ONE

INTRODUCTION

THIS YEAR IN REVIEW is brought to you by Pfizer, FTX, and Raytheon.

Every year I write an annual survey of what happened in the world. After posting at Peak Prosperity, it gets a bump from the putative commies at Zerohedge,[1,2,3,4] whom I read religiously. (I have made over sixty cameo appearances at Zerohedge, consistent with being booted off Twitter four times.)

Why do I write it? My best answer is that you do not understand something until you have written your ideas down coherently. I am also trying to figure out who keeps yelling "Beetlejuice!"

> Write as often as possible, not with the idea at once of getting into print, but as if you were learning an instrument.
>
> — J. B. Priestley, English novelist

I break every rule of blog marketing; nobody writes just one gigantic blog post a year. But it makes the rounds. It is onerous and exhausting, especially since I must necessarily procrastinate up to the deadline.

Most years, I write what I can and then wrap it. In 2021, however, I had a primal drive to cover the usual stuff plus two topics that do not lend themselves to abbreviation: the COVID pandemic and rising global authoritarianism. Many are now realizing that the former is a manifestation of the latter. While I may not have been correct, I had to get it right ... if that makes any sense. Like so many young athletes in 2021, I left it all on the field. I uploaded it but was too demoralized and depressed to send it to friends, confidants, or family.

Diehards found it anyway, and sent their comments. Two, whom I consider good friends, had diametric views that I will take the liberty of paraphrasing. Sitting on one shoulder was Tony Deden, founder of Edelweiss Holdings (based in Switzerland) and a saint, who sensed my pain and urged me to stop writing. He went beyond the pale by inviting me to detox in his chalet in the Swiss Alps or on his 25-acre strawberry farm on Crete. I had to pass because traveling is hard on the family. On the other shoulder was David Einhorn, a friend of a dozen years, who has helped me in ways few will ever know. He told me I *must* keep writing it.

I think 2021 could have been the apex, and a perfect time to stop. I sided with David this year but may soon follow Tony's advice.

OK, Dave, but what is that peeing thing about? Well, I was scheduled to host David and his lovely girlfriend, Natalie, for a late dinner on a Thursday night at my house. I answered the door in my bathrobe, saw their horrified looks, and exclaimed, "Fuck. Is it Thursday?" We got takeout and all was fine, even after my sweet little Boston Terrier puppy, Fiona, pissed on Natalie. *That*, dear friends, is how you treat financial royalty!

All roads lead to Ukraine. Trying to understand the war from a dead cold start was monumentally hard. Geopolitical events occur in order to teach Americans geography; I am no exception.

As a combination of foreshadowing and trigger warning, I am going to steelman the debate by taking a decidedly Russian perspective, although I am unsure if it qualifies as steelmanning if you come to believe it. If this will drive you nuts, I beg you to stop reading, because you will just get mad while I wallow in the slime of your frustrated soul.

> I propose Vladimir Putin for the Nobel Prize in Medicine, for solving COVID globally in 48 hours.
>
> — Anonymous

As Ron Popeil would have said, "But wait. There's more!" The Ukrainian theme runs deeper than that. Here is a little more foreshadowing.

Canadian trucker crusher Chrystia Freeland has deep Ukrainian Nazi roots. Nina Jankowicz, former head of Biden's Orwellian "Disinformation Governance Board" (Ministry of Truth, for short) was doing psy-ops work in Ukraine in her previous gig. The collapse of the world's second-largest cryptocurrency exchange (FTX) revealed a massive money laundering scheme through Ukraine, with political ties in the U.S. The rising tide of a global neo-Nazism—an idea I am still dubious about—connects tiki torchers in Charlottesville, suspicious rabble-rousers in the "insurrection" of January 6, 2021, the Patriot Front, and the Azov Battalion in Ukraine.[5]

Who is that guy with the horns, hanging out with a Ukrainian "nationalist"?

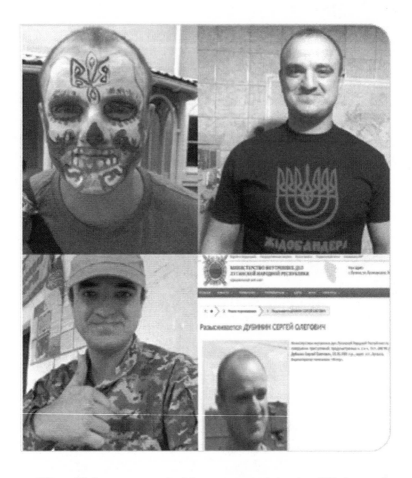

The U.S.-sponsored bioweapons lab in Wuhan that spawned the SARS-CoV-2 virus has 36 counterparts in Ukraine. The crackhead son of the President of the United States ran scams in Ukraine via Burisma Holdings, the same country in which his dad funded a proxy war. And which country was the largest donor to the Clinton Foundation for 15 years? Ukraine. Go figure.

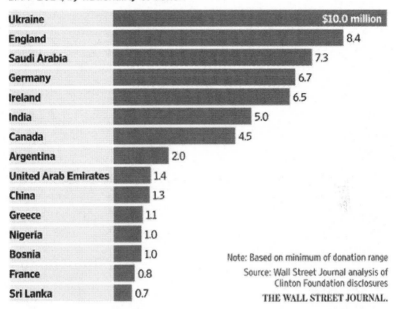

Foreign Donors

Contributions by individuals of more than $50,000 to Clinton Foundation, 1999-2014, by nationality of donor:

Ukraine	$10.0 million
England	8.4
Saudi Arabia	7.3
Germany	6.7
Ireland	6.5
India	5.0
Canada	4.5
Argentina	2.0
United Arab Emirates	1.4
China	1.3
Greece	1.1
Nigeria	1.0
Bosnia	1.0
France	0.8
Sri Lanka	0.7

Note: Based on minimum of donation range

Source: Wall Street Journal analysis of Clinton Foundation disclosures

THE WALL STREET JOURNAL.

A Year in Transition. This was my runner-up for the title of this Year in Review (YIR). Aren't we always stuck on the "Möbius strip from hell" that never ends? Francis Fukuyama and Tom Friedman were wrong: history did not end, and the world is going spherical again rather quickly.

Of course, we never know the future, but each year seems to have themes that play out, with a quantized feel to it. By contrast, 2022 has left world economies heading south but with no bottom in sight. Neither the Federal Reserve Bank nor the markets are done inflicting pain. The risk of worldwide famine is real, but with inestimable consequences. The futures of Bitcoin and other cryptocurrencies hang in the balance, with more than just price corrections now in play. The war in

Ukraine could end with a whimper (if Russia wins) or with a thermonuclear conflagration (where nobody wins). Europeans are pondering the relative merits of freezing to death owing to energy shortages or starving to death owing to food shortages, but maybe those potentially biblical events are merely clickbait. The World Economic Forum (WEF) has reared its ugly head—its Great Reset is not just a theory—yet we still haven't a clue what those diabolical authoritarian meat puppets are up to. Why do we have to start eating bugs and forfeiting all earthly belongings? And forfeiting them to whom?

> *Me, by email:* [blah blah, blah ... we are hosed ... blah, blah, gurgle, gurgle].
>
> *Larry Summers:* Thanks for these thoughtful comments. I mostly agree.
>
> *Stephen Roach:* Thanks, Dave. I am in violent agreement with Larry these days. Under Powell, the Fed is currently in the deepest hole it has ever been in. Anything is possible, I guess—including a nighttime landing on an aircraft carrier in the midst of a raging typhoon. Might not be soft, though.

Maybe the markets and the economy will be fine—maybe I am merely full of shit—but the other guys in that email threesome are deep and dark too. Stephen, who has been so generous with his time and wisdom over many years, expressed dismay in an op-ed over a particularly inaccurate call about what would happen. I offered wisdom in return.

> *Me, by email:* Several years ago I promised myself I would stop reading about what *will* happen. I am

not sure we ever know what *had* happened and am clueless about what *is* happening.

Roach: You are a better man than me!

My accrued wisdom comes from having read and made too many predictions that were garbage, or profoundly early. I have spent countless hours over the years pondering alternative narratives via suppositories offered in the press: good versus evil, the meaning of life, contemporary events in historical contexts, and what it means to be human. The future is too much to handle.

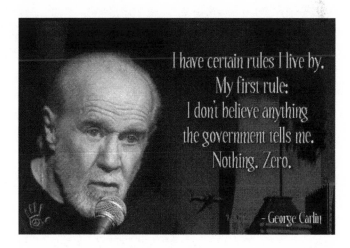

Michael Crichton once noted that it is sobering to read newspapers from thirty years ago; the above-the-fold hot topics seem so irrelevant. He also pointed out that persistent fear can lay waste to your mental and physical health.[6]

I identify as a conspiracy theorist. My pronouns are: They/Lied.

> When there's no such thing as truth, you can't
> define reality. When you can't define reality, the
> only thing that matters is power.
>
> — Maajid Nawaz, British activist and radio host

I am confounded that I—openly right of center, and thus in a group comprising less than two percent of Cornell University's faculty—am trying to warn the rest of my colleagues that they are being duped by evil corporations in collusion with Big Government—the definition of fascism. Too much acid in middle school for this boy, I guess.

Despite my growing doubts that I may never penetrate the layers of the onion where truth resides, my resolve (which has strengthened over the last couple of years) is that whenever something of importance seems off or confusing, your default position should be that somebody in a position of power is conspiring. Why? Because that is what people in power do. It is in their DNA. They wake up every morning pondering how many baby harp seals they can bludgeon that day.

Give me *any* topic—a keyword, even—and I can serve up an alternative model that will not be told on CNN. My training as a parent tells me those demons are scheming. So, indeed, *I am a conspiracy theorist.* If you are not, ignorance is bliss. Hang on to those lovely thoughts. Those who always default to incompetence as the explanation appear not to be under the spell of the little green gremlins who crawl out of my cell phone and molest me while I sleep.

The True Believer. In 1953, the formerly homeless Eric
Hoffer[7] wrote *The True Believer,*[8] a short and highly digestible
story of mass movements—why they start, where they get their
oxygen from, how they end, and who the critical players are.
The book got into my DNA. Not to be a plot spoiler, but
Hoffer's ideas are too important to count on you visiting
Amazon.

> You can discover what your enemy fears most by
> observing the means he uses to frighten you.
>
> — Eric Hoffer

Mass movements start with intellectuals, often in
universities, where most bad ideas are hatched. The movement
gets oxygen when the masses—Hoffer calls them "the fanatics"—
pick up the ball and run with it. He serves up an unflattering
view of the fanatics as societal bottom feeders with little to lose
from profound change. "Fuck it; let's do it!" They feel
important; part of a glorious army, fighting for a righteous cause
against villains who are the root cause of the wretchedness of
their existence. They don't want freedom; they want freedom
from responsibility. The rallying cry is always about a promised
future that will be a return to a once-glorious past. Make

America Great Again. Battle-scarred soldiers returning home and searching for something familiar and elevating may embrace militias.

Friend and author, Peter Boghossian, reminds us that you will not sway fanatics with facts, but rather by understanding where they are coming from emotionally.[9]

> Our greatest pretenses are built up not to hide the evil and the ugly in us, but our emptiness. The hardest thing to hide is something that is not there.
>
> — Eric Hoffer

At his most poignant, Hoffer notes that there is often self-sacrifice involved, whether it is ancient clerics giving up all Earthly belongings (including sex) or climate changers giving up their cars (and maybe sex). They need to feel their suffering is not wasted.

> Propaganda does not deceive people; it merely helps them to deceive themselves.
>
> — Eric Hoffer

Artful leaders will sense the direction in which the masses are moving, and then lead them there. Their tools include imitation, hatred, and propaganda. We must conform (mask up), hate the opponent (Donald or Hillary), and tell the noble lie (vaccinate, for the children). Propaganda doesn't flip natural tendencies, only amplifies existing ones.

Sometimes a movement peters out. Other times it ends in a tragedy measurable in millions of lost lives. Oddly, many are more willing to die for an abstract future than to protect rights and material goods they already possess.

> "One of the saddest lessons of history is this: If we've been bamboozled long enough, we tend to reject any evidence of the bamboozle. We're no longer interested in finding out the truth. The bamboozle has captured us. It's simply too painful to acknowledge, even to ourselves, that we've been taken. Once you give a charlatan power over you, you almost never get it back."
> — Carl Sagan,
> The Demon-Haunted World

A clever leader can head the mob off at the pass. A potentially brilliant example, Malcolm X, inserted Islam—not my favourite religion, I should say—to bring meaning to otherwise meaningless lives. I have a theory that FDR was an insider—shocking, I know—who recognized that fanatical Trotskyites would win if Amity Shlaes' *Forgotten Man* was left adrift. By compromising bigly and contrary to right-wing dogma, FDR saved capitalism.

But beware: disillusioned fanatics don't just move to the middle but rather flip to the opposite pole, retaining their fanaticism. The "true believers" are addicted to movements; they are serial zealots. I catch glimpses of this when looking in the mirror. I think of myself as a "True Disbeliever." Give me a narrative and I will find the other side, but am I simply joining a different mob? Probably, but at least it is usually a less populous mob.

> Passionate hatred can give meaning and purpose to an empty life.
>
> — Eric Hoffer

With social media and hordes of unhappy campers noticing massive wealth disparity, we have entered the Golden Age of Fanaticism. The Forgotten Man has reappeared. While reading Hoffer's 70-year-old treatise, I could see it everywhere—MAGA, Trump haters, Antifa, climate changers, vaxxers, anti-vaxxers, maskers, Bitcoin hodlers, pro-choicers and pro-lifers, Black Lives Matter, tiki torchers, or spotted-owl savers. Will this era end with an FDR or a Josef Stalin?

MY YEAR

I HAVE THE RIGHT to remain silent. I just don't have the ability.

From twelve years of tradition and a need to chronicle my life before my adult-onset progeria causes me to hit my expiration date or lose one marble too many, I go through Dave's Year. It is like a diary.

High points in 2022 included a hedge fund founders' dinner in NYC. I don't remember ever founding a hedge fund, but there I was in a midtown Manhattan rathskeller, dining with about eight guys whose net worths were comfortably larger than mine. I watched a legend with battle scars wrestle a tech bull (calf) to the dirt, declaring, "Do you know what a ninety-five percent correction is? It's a ninety percent correction that then cuts in half!" I got this odd sense that many of their profound skills ran deep but were siloed.

When asked for our outside-the-box idea at dinner's end, I went with "Russian oil companies." A week later I made my move. Two days later Putin made *his* move, and two seconds later the shares stopped trading. Fortunately, I had sized my position brilliantly—so small that it did not matter—because I was looking to catch the dead cat, not the falling knife.

It is possible that they will reappear when Wall Street decides it's time. Nevertheless, the dinner guests got a chuckle.

I am told that my writeup on COVID in the 2021 YIR [1] was considered by Steve Scalise's staff for uploading to the Congressional record: "I will send this to my staff on the Select Subcommittee on the Coronavirus. They will be able to pull a lot of gems out of this. #2 — My staff is excited to get this data, and they're combing through it." I have no idea if it made it, but I savor Pyrrhic victories.

I also get my share of unsolicited gifts—"schwag" as it is called—including heaps of books from authors, a sweater, a set of Wiseguy suspenders,[2] a hat saying "Vaccine Survivor", Epstein coffee mugs, two hundred Ivermectin tablets, and a few silver rounds. I'm holding out for ingots and cash. Gold would be great but rhodium is my first choice.

By doing long-form podcasts with Chris Irons (Quoth The Raven), I learned that keeping an empty glass nearby enables me to go on for hours without a formal break. This year I also learned that if you are drinking copious amounts of ginger ale, *do not get distracted.* It was Gandhi time.

Podcasts. I do tons of podcasts. Talking to smart people is a hoot, and if they want to record it and post it on the internet, I am up with that. (I have many more phone calls.) They are all good. The irony is that I can bust my ass to get two thousand people to click on a paper in the *Journal of the American Chemical Society* but get over a quarter-million clicks from a two-hour podcast with Tony "Pomp" Pompliano.

Largely for archival reasons, I list the podcasts below, with links.

While not wishing to offend any host, I will highlight a couple. The three-hour Twitter Spaces with the legendary George Noble (Peter Lynch's understudy) was honorific. The podcast with Tony Pomp from a cabin in the Adirondacks seems to have captured the public's imagination the most.[3] Two foursomes with Tommy Carrigan, Tom Luongo, and Jim Kunstler are raucous.[4,5] A scheduled Newsmax interview was cut short when one of Biden's drone attacks hit his target and me with one shot.

The New Orleans Investor Conference in October, filled with old friends and bucket listers, included four independent speaking gigs. Sometimes I wonder through what wormhole I exited the organic chemistry universe and entered the politico-economic universe. Curiously, a self-evidently black limo driver who drove me through the murder capital of the U.S.[6] to the hotel had exited his own wormhole to become one hundred percent MAGA. I wrote about the rising tide of black conservatism in 2016; he assured me I was correct.[7]

Podcasts in 2022

George Noble, marathon Twitter Spaces.[8]

2022 New Orleans Investment Conference[9] Boom and Bust panel[10] with Jim Stack, Peter Boockvar (@pboockvar), and Jim Iuorio (@jimiuorio).

2022 New Orleans Investment talk: The Merits of Price Gouging.[11]

2021 New Orleans Investment Conference round table (released 2022).[12]

Justin O'Connell (@GoldSilverBTC), the GoldSilverBitcoin show.[13]

George Gammon (@GeorgeGammon), The Rebel Capitalist Show,[14] with a few short clips.[15,16,17,18]

Elijah Johnson on the Liberty and Finance podcast (two).[19,20]

Jay Martin (@JayMartin) of the Jay Martin Show.[21]

Tom Bodrovics (@PalisadesRadio) on Palisades Gold Radio.[22]

James Kunstler (@jhkunstler) on KunstlerCast.[23]

Tommy Carrigan (@tommys_podcast) of Tommy's Podcast, with Tom Luongo (@TFL1728).[24]

Tommy's Podcast, in February 2022.[25]

Tommy's Podcast, in May 2022.[26]

Tommy's Podcast, with James Kunstler and Tom Luongo, in August 2022.[27]

Tommy's Podcast, with James Kunstler and Tom Luongo, in November 2022.[28]

Tom Luongo of Gold Goats 'n Guns.[29]

Craig Hemke (#TFMetals) of the TFMetals Podcast.[30]

Marty Bent (@MartyBent) on Tales from the Crypt.[31]

Jim Iuorio (@jimiuorio) and Bob Iaccino (@Bob_Iaccino) on Futures Edge.[32,33]

Crypto Highlights.[34]

Anthony Pomp (@APompliano).[35]

My Zoom group (Medical Doctors for Covid Ethics International) (starts at 25 minutes).[36]

Michael St. Pierre; Stand-Easy with MSP.[37]

Kai Hoffmann of Soar Financial (August 2022).[38]

Kai Hoffman of SF Live interview (October 2022).[39]

Lee Justo (@Lee_Justo) of Risk.[40]

Cedric Youngelman (@CedYoungelman) of The Bitcoin Matrix.[41]

West Virginia radio show, "Us & Them".[42]

Anthony Fatseas (@AnthonyFatseas) on WTFinance.[43]

Tom Pochari.[44,45,46]

Tyler Chesser (@thetylerchesser) on Elevate.[47,48]

Four TradKatKnight podcasts (behind a paywall) that I've never listened to.

> I mean, they say you die twice. One time when you stop breathing and a second time, a bit later on, when somebody says your name for the last time.
>
> — Banksy [49]

Reviews of previous years. I have to do a little housekeeping. Website rollovers and general internet rot has damaged links to twelve consecutive Reviews. A fully repaired, comprehensive list is here [50] and is listed below. This is merely archival, hoping somebody will keep uttering my name even if only to curse me.

I have many good friends on Twitter. Here on the next page are two of the toughest hombres on Twitter.

Marc Cohodes @AlderLaneEggs · 17m   ···
There is Me.... There is @EpsilonTheory , there is @fleckcap and
@DavidBCollum

> ● **Billy The Goat** @Billygoatcryto · 18m
>
> Replying to @AlderLaneEggs @andrewrsorkin and @zerohedge
>
> The question is: who's there to ask those questions? Is there anyone
> with the people's interests in mind?

The_Real_Fly   ···
@The_Real_Fly

I love @DavidBCollum

1:47 AM · Aug 28, 2022 · Twitter for iPhone

Mr. Fly is well-known on financial Twitter, or fintwit. Marc is a famous short seller who went supernova in the mainstream press by calling out FTX a month before the collapse. (Marc: my offer for dinner on my deck still stands. Same holds for you, Mr. Fly, but I'm not a floosie.)

Before moving onto the specific issues I should mention fact-checkers. They started with a husband and wife team at Snopes that, over time, was putting out more content than theoretically possible for a twosome. They have proliferated across the internet like Tribbles, and have mutated into propaganda machines. Fact-checkers get things right only when it is politically expedient to do so. If you take what they say at face value, you are an idiot, and that's a fact.[64]

My immutable law of fact-checking is that the more you find, the more likely it is that the so-called conspiracy theory being debunked is correct. My allusions to fact-checkers throughout this book are, without exception, to be viewed as a vote of confidence that the idea being checked is correct.

The truth is like a lion; you don't have to defend it.
Let it loose; it will defend itself.

— Saint Augustine of Hippo

INVESTING

There is time to go long, time to go short, and time to go fishing.

— Jesse Livermore, the most famous trader

AS I SAY EVERY YEAR, I will be fine in retirement as long as I do not fuck up. The problem is that inflation now massively increases the probability of fucking up. You can't sit on cash for too long without serious erosion of its value, but more people have died reaching for yield than at the point of a gun. There are treacherous waters ahead.

Replaying the tape so y'all understand how I got here, I had three great decades and one dawg. I was 100 percent long bonds, getting about 12 percent annualized, from 1980 up to the '87 crash. The crash, and a chat with a colleague, caused me to flip to equities. Shocking to those who know me, I became a raging equity bull—a tech bull—until about July of '98, when market valuations made me too nervous: I pulled half of my equities out.

Following the Asian crisis, some dumb luck with trivial back-of-the-envelope calculations convinced me that we had rallied back into an epic bubble. I decided that leaving even half my equities exposed had been stupid, and pulled the rest out in mid-1999. (Pulling the trigger on my soaring tech stocks took cojones.)

I went long cash and gold in '99. White-knuckling it through the 2001 bottom was hard, but I haven't sold an ounce to date. Hoping to hedge inflation, I bought quite a bit of Fidelity energy and material funds starting in 2001, leading to an amazing (graded on a curve) 13 percent annualized return for the decade ending on December 31, 2009.

> The market does what it should do, just not always when.
>
> — Jesse Livermore

After three decades of good calls, Mr. SmartyPants then failed to anticipate the Fed having trillions of acts of sex with barnyard animals to mitigate what should have been a deeper plunge in 2008–09. *I did not ride the 'roid rage up to 2021.* While the world partied like it was 1999, I rode what Dylan Grice called his "cockroach portfolio: 25 percent stocks, 25 percent bonds, 25 percent cash, and 25 percent gold" but with a lower equity weighting, clawing out a four percent annualized gain in total net worth.

I forgive myself. One of the greatest bull runs happened, but it never should have. I can hear the bulls cackling about "what is versus what should be." However, I think the next secular bear market has started and will take years to finish. Being right this time will not be that satisfying. "The vanquished cry but the victors do not laugh."

> The age of financial assets is over.
>
> — Murray Stahl, Horizon Kinetics

At the urging of some luminaries, who suggested my portfolio was a little out of balance (psychotically so), I saw opportunities in energy in 2020 as it dropped to just two percent of the S&P, Exxon was replaced in the Dow by Salesforce.com, and nuclear power could glow in the dark some day. (Exxon is up 83 percent since the swap while Salesforce.com is down 49 percent.)

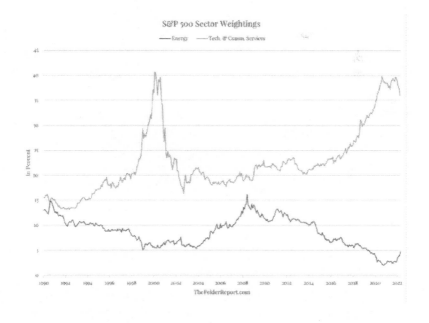

If 2020 was the energy bottom, I nailed it. The gains shown below do not even include substantial dividends. I did not size the energy move right, but it was enough to make a difference. I think we are entering a commodity and energy boom that may last decades, owing to decades of underinvestment that may persist as governments oppose fossil fuels on "ethical" grounds.[1]

You might want to buy the companies that already have pipes and mines in place, approximating royalty trusts. Grantham says such companies are 60 percent cheap, relative to the S&P.[2] (I prefer absolute valuations, not those based on a curve relative to other bubbles.) Murray Stahl, a very impressive maven at Horizon Kinetics, sees a 25-year cycle dead ahead as the age of finance for the sake of finance tanks.[3] I intend to give them some money to play with, but not yet.

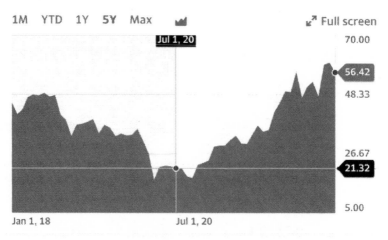

Fidelity FSENX energy fund

I live on Cayuga Lake, in a house that is a lifestyle changer. But it is three times bigger than I need, which forces me to call it a real estate play. Cash in the Teachers Insurance and

Annuity Association (TIAA) and other short-term bonds is returning 3.5 percent. I also have 15 percent of my wealth in a fund that is not under my control (white privilege from my parents) in an old-man 40:60 portfolio, with both portions getting beaten up (minus 12 percent, year to date). My risk assets and their 2022 returns are as follows.

- Fidelity Select Gold Portfolio (FSAGX): +11%.
- Fidelity Natural Resources Fund (FNARX): +35%.
- Fidelity Select Energy Portfolio (FSENX): +58%.
- Goehring & Rozencwajg Resources (GRHIX): +15%.
- Impala Platinum (IMPUY): –18%.
- Jaguar Mining (JAGGF): –40%.
- Kirkland Lake (KL): +8%.
- Palm Valley Capital Fund (PVCMX): +2%.
- Rio Tinto (RIO): +3%.
- Sibanye Stillwater Limited (SBSW): –12%.
- Sprott Physical Silver Trust (PSLV): +3%.
- RSX: –100%.
- Central Fund of Canada: 0%.
- Gold: 0%.
- Silver: +3%.

Many of these positions have fortress balance sheets and huge dividends (not included above), making them buy-and-holds as long as the dividends continue to be paid. Owing to the relative weightings of all assets (not shown), dividends, and net savings (21 percent of my gross salary, contributing 0.8 percent to that gain), my 2022 year-to-date wealth accrual came in at 0.5 percent. Graded on a curve, that's pretty good. But throw in inflation and I got whacked.

Let's walk through some of the thinking. I have a small position in Eric Cinnamond's PVCMX. Eric is a brilliant micro-cap investor. He had closed his fund but then reopened it in 2019. He listens to hundreds of conference calls, shows no interest in hot tips, and invests when he sees the whites of their eyes. The chart below is revealing. It is flat for the first nine months because he bought *nothing*. Eric nearly bottom-called the March 2020 COVID dip and then went flat again. He is currently *80 percent* cash equivalents. I am paying him for his patience and will give him more when I see activity pick up.

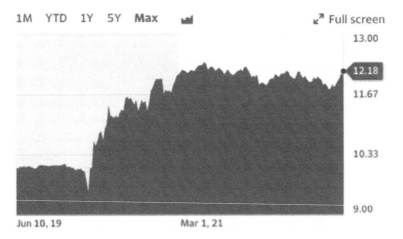

Palm Valley Capital Fund (PVCMX)

Goehring and Rozencwajg's GRHIX is a uranium play. It is long-term (decades), but these guys seem to know the below-the-radar small miners. So far, so good. I ticked that position up a little this year but it is not chunky yet. As Europe and the rest of the world get pounded by energy shortages, people may soon be begging for nuclear power plants in their backyards—NIMBY turns RIMBY (right in my backyard).

As for the other energy issues, I will leave that to the section on Energy and Ukraine. Rio Tinto has all the attributes I like, and it would require an asteroid to take out its worldwide mining operations. Even if the Environmental, Social, and Governance (ESG) movement goes wild and everybody turns to alternative energies, gigatons of basic metals must then be pulled out of the ground, arguably way more than known reserves.[4] This superimposes nicely on Russia's diminished contributions to commodity supplies.

Russia's Commodities Reach
The share of Russian exports that go to each destination

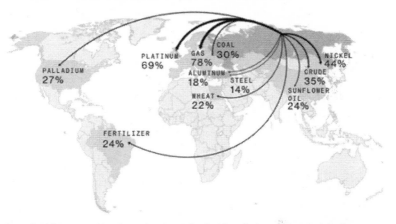

Note: Coal figures combine thermal and metallurgical; liquefied natural gas and pipeline gas are also combined.

Sources: UN Comtrade Database (metals); International Energy Agency (coal); UN's Food and Agriculture Organization (wheat; sunflower oil); Joint Organisations Data Initiative; Bloomberg; Eurostat; BP; (crude); Trade Data Monitor; Green Markets, a Bloomberg company (fertilizer); BP (gas)

> The game of nominal value of money is over, as this system does not allow to control the supply of resources ... Our product, our rules. We don't play by the rules we didn't create.[5]
>
> — Alexei Miller, Gazprom CEO

The three platinum miners (IMPUY, SBSW, and ANGPY) have strong balance sheets, handsome dividends, no tailwind from a stagnant platinum spot price, and valuations like Russian equities. They are, however, in South Africa, where the confiscation of assets is by no means a zero-probability event [6,7] and labor issues are always present.[8,9]

The founder of a fund professing to be the largest private holder of one of the above three gave me a two-hour phone tutorial. Critically, these platinum miners are making their money off rhodium. Unidentified shoppers are stealing catalytic converters from cars (including my son's).[10] SBSW is actively investing in new production.[11] Above-ground platinum supplies have been cut in half in one year.[12] The hydrogen fuel cells could be game changers, and they use lots of platinum.[13]

The risk is that Goldman has a "buy" recommendation on the miners, said to be based on good fundamentals, which probably means they have shares and ingots to unload onto suckers.[14]

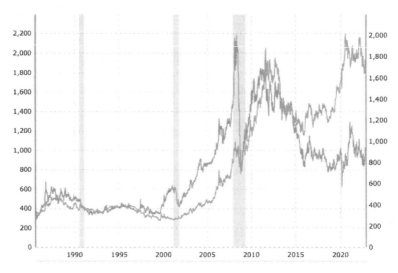

Platinum (blue) versus gold (orange), USD per ounce [15]

I had a token position in the Russian equity fund RSX for years, but was interested in a bigger position. RSX was loaded with Lukoil, PhosAgro, Sberbank, and Gazprom, all priced like used pillows at a Salvation Army thrift store. Some very smart guys were speaking of Russian energy companies as contrarian plays in 2021. Then Vlad decided to threaten Ukraine, and those shares started selling hard. Although rare bulls such as Harris "Kuppy" Kupperman saw the contrarian play of a lifetime, most shareholders wanted out. Kentucky's pension plan was a huge holder,[16] which is *the* most contrary indicator because everything they touch turns to shit.

I pulled the trigger on another token amount—less than 0.1 percent of my net worth—as the shares dropped to about 20 percent of net asset value, with a price/earnings ratio below two, hoping to go full goblin if geopolitical tensions subsided. A couple of days later, trading in all Russian assets was terminated and the margin calls on the big players came rolling in.[17]

So are my RSX shares gone for good? I am not sure. It's like a Cuban expat living in Miami and holding a land deed in Cuba—a dollar and a dream. As it stands, by terminating trading in the shares, we essentially handed the ownership of companies holding vast resources back to the Rooskies. Does that make any sense?

Meanwhile, JPMorgan and Bank of America continued quietly trading Russian bonds.[18] I'm not sure how that works, but it tells me that trading in equity shares will resume when Wall Street says so. Kuppy *et al.* could emerge as big winners. Blackrock and Goldman will get first dibs after that. I will not be given a cheap entry, which means my token loss will become a token gain.

GOLD AND SILVER

> I'm a fan of gold. I think gold's valuable in a crisis. The market has come to believe in an omniscient Federal Reserve, and it's no such thing. These guys don't really know what they're doing in any deep way. It's a giant financial experiment, and we're at the mercy of their experiment that maybe is right now in the process of going wrong, so God help us.

— Seth Klarman, Baupost

Having entered the World of Peter Schiff—every imaginable disaster that Peter envisioned was teed up—gold had a nice start but did very little over the year. One should not, however, be discouraged. Over the last two decades, gold has climbed 9.1 percent annualized (see below), which is impressive for a pet rock.

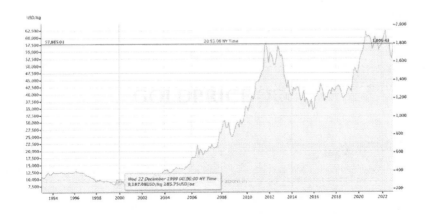

Gold price, 1994–2022

I can hear you say, "Yeah. But who owned gold (or silver) for two decades?" The answer is: me, and about five other guys. I should probably draw readers' attention to Incrementum's reports, which are eye candy for the bugs and a primer for bugs-in-training.[1,2]

What is holding gold back? Possibly the crypto "hodlers"—those who "hold on for dear life"—are sapping demand for alternative currency equivalents, but they haven't exactly benefitted from a strong bid, with Bitcoin down 59 percent year to date and 72 percent off its all-time high. I can entertain the idea that the powerful (supra-sovereign level) are rigging the gold market, but I am not convinced of it.[3]

In related news, JPM got its annual "tax the rich" wrist slap for committing massive fraud in the gold futures markets.[4,5] "This was an open strategy on the desk. It wasn't hidden." However, I remain unconvinced that they are *suppressing* the price rather than simply running over investors on both the upside and downside.

The globally destabilizing U.S. dollar strength in the forex currency markets certainly hurt the gold price in USD, but gold denominated in all other currencies has done well. However, the USD is still getting trampled if we stop grading on the forex curve (see Inflation).

The above-ground gold supplies from mining are growing at only 1–2 percent annualized. With gold demand being sopped up by ETFs, it strikes me as possible that for gold to take off it may require price discovery in which the physical market overwhelms the futures market by forcing a default at the Comex, which seems plausible in a world that becomes more dystopian.

Goldman raised its price target to $2,500 an ounce,[6] which is, as noted, a contrary indicator.

> Companies whose profits are so undermined will likely see their share prices drop ... Another way to defend the purchasing power of your savings if we return to an era of price controls is by investing in gold.[7]
>
> — Russell Napier, legendary deflationist of yore

There were a few memorable moments in the gold markets. Uganda was said to have discovered deposits capable of producing 320,000 tons (OK, tonnes) of finished product[8] to increase the above-ground global supply by 200 percent. The market didn't even flicker at that ridiculous claim.

The 2014 CIA-sponsored coup in Ukraine and the subsequent invasion of Crimea elicited the generous offer by the U.S. to take possession of $12 billion of Ukrainian gold for safekeeping. In 2022 the U.S. shipment of money and weapons led to the generous U.S. offer to take ownership.[9,10,11] We seem to scoop up this barbarous relic, every chance we get.

The Ukrainian debacle, including confiscation of anything remotely Slavic, has revealed to Russia and all those paying attention that the U.S. dollar may be an undependable reserve currency. Russia and China have been amassing gold steadily for most of the last two decades.

In an interview that caused my eyes to bulge like those of a cartoon character, Simon Hunt estimated that the putative 8,500 tons of gold owned by the U.S. may be dwarfed by 12,000 tons of Roosky gold and 55,000 tons of gold in China,[12] of which 12,000 are owned by the public.[13] State-owned corporations have warehouses bulging with stashes. At the very end of 2022, evidence of a big buyer—a gold whale—was traced to China.

> I believe it would be both risk-reducing and return-enhancing to consider adding gold to one's portfolio.
>
> — Ray Dalio, Bridgewater Associates

Silver was tame, too (see below). As with gold, the 9.2 percent annualized 20-year return is nothing to sneeze at. Above-ground silver supplies are said to be dropping,[14] but I have been hearing variants of that story for my 23 years of ownership. The global effort to squander resources on sketchy sources of energy such as solar panels is a reason for optimism. Silver is in every electronic device, including contemporary solar panels, and embedded deeply enough to be uneconomic to recycle at current prices, especially in the Western world.[15]

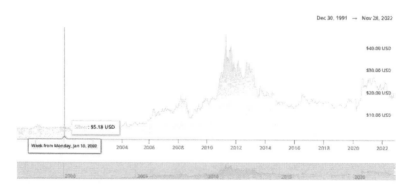

Silver price per ounce, 2000-22 [16]

> Our central case is a hard landing by the end of '23 ... I don't rule out something really bad ... We are

in deep trouble ... the repercussions of that are going to be with us for a long, long time.[17]

— Stan Druckenmiller, God

THE ECONOMY

THE GLOBAL ECONOMY is too much in flux to predict even six months out. While many leading economic indicators are sloping downward, the Fed is hiking interest rates and has used the word "pain." Pivot watchers think the Fed will chicken out, but I think they intend to bring the system to its knees. A hard landing will look like a yard sale—broken and useless shit everywhere—but will also be an emergent process, in which the details of the wreckage cannot possibly be foreseen. If it is accompanied by deglobalization—if the global players continue to be uncooperative—it could get *really* ugly.

Peter Zeihan, an ex-Stratfor demographer mentioned further below, says that a profound deglobalization is an inevitable consequence of demographics.[1] Putin and NATO are accelerating the process, and it could collapse with one bone-headed move. Meanwhile, the Covidians are preparing the Hofferian fanatics for the next lockdown.

> This economic crisis is just beginning, and it's going to be as bad or worse and as long as it was during the 1970s.
>
> — Peter Navarro, former White House economic advisor

Before largely taking a pass this year and watching the economy play out, I would like to take a shot at the question that has plagued many: where have all the workers gone? It is like going into the woods and finding no squirrels or birds. Some economists have called this a strong labor market. I might concede that it is tight, but broken is more accurate.

Seven million American men of prime working age—25 to 54 years—are not merely out of work, but are not even looking for work.

It is being called the Great Resignation. When you ask small business and restaurant owners where their former employees have gone, they respond with some variant of "working for somebody else." I have not found these mysterious employers of lower-wage workers.

Somehow there is a lack of price discovery between workers and potential employers. There may be multiple reasons for the missing workers.

- Illegal aliens went home and did not come back.
- People sat on their decks pounding brewskis during the lockdown, and decided that retiring or living on one salary is not so bad.
- Disabilities, real or perceived, have arisen.
- Some workers have joined what I call the less productive part of the workforce, which includes bloggers, Substackers, and YouTubers looking for patrons. Others are, as one trucker told me, "trading Bitcoin."
- Cops have quit because they now hate their jobs at the very moment when (or because) crime in the cities is spiking.
- Mom-and-pop businesses were destroyed by the lockdown policies of Fauci *et al.*
- Moms or dads who home-schooled their kids are now savvy enough to recognize that marginally offsetting daycare costs with a second salary is common core-level math and economics (makes no sense).
- Some died from COVID and what is euphemistically called "excess mortality" (vaccines).

The Ethical Skeptic, an anonymous and impressive blogger and COVID analyst, compiled 42 reasons behind Johnny Paycheck's hit song, "Take This Job and Shove It." [2] It will require wage increases, severe economic hardships, or simply maxing out all credit lines to pull the workers back to the workforce. Paradoxically, workers needing wage gains will be inflationary.

INFLATION

> Stagflation is going to kill you.
>
> — Rebecca Patterson, chief investment strategist at Bridgewater Associates

> Hyperinflation is going to change everything. It's happening.
>
> —Jack Dorsey (@jack), CEO and founder of Twitter, on November 22, 2021

AT THE HEDGE-FUND FOUNDERS' DINNER that I mentioned above, only one attendee convinced me that he understood that inflation had reverse-transcribed itself into our DNA and was hunkered down. The rest seemed to believe that the Fed would throw a switch and inflation would be vanquished—Bernanke-style. Society seems to have forgotten that many of the most horrid events in history followed on the heels of destructive inflations. Rudy Havenstein understands.[1]

> Inflation is a worldwide problem right now because of a war in Iraq ... excuse me, the war in Ukraine. I'm thinking about Iraq because that's where my son died.[2]
>
> — Joe Biden, talking about Bethesda, Iraq

Our leaders' qualifications seem undeniable. We have a president who noted that a rise from 8.2 to 8.3 percent is OK because it is just "an inch" (putting thumb and forefinger close together) and a vice president who thinks that the slight increase means there is almost no inflation. Meanwhile, Congress passed a bill of nearly half a trillion dollars to fight inflation, and then allocated the money to climate change grifters and to grow the IRS secret police by 87,000.[3]

Am I the only one who sees the Grim Reaper in the IRS logo?

I'm sick of this stuff! The American people think the reason for inflation is the government spending more money. Simply not true!

—Joe Biden

It's important to dispel some of those who say, well, it's the government spending. No, it isn't. The government spending is doing the exact reverse, reducing the national debt. It is not inflationary.

—Nancy Pelosi

> The people in Washington will tell you inflation is produced by greedy businessmen or it's produced by grasping trade unions or it's produced by spendthrift consumers or maybe it's those terrible Arab sheiks ... only money has that printing press and, therefore, only Washington can produce inflation.[4]

— Milton Friedman

Majority of Americans back new stimulus checks to combat inflation

Khaleda Rahman

October 30, 2022

Ron Paul warned us for years that government spending is the problem, as did Milton Friedman. Davy Crockett had his come-to-Jesus moment in his legendary speech to Congress ("It is not yours to give"),[5] in which he apologized for voting for a big recovery act.

Never have so many owed so much to so few. The quirky genius Kim Dotcom reminded us what economist Larry Kotlikoff[6] has been sounding the alarm about: even if you were to sell all factories, real estate, hard assets, and equities—a complete liquidation at *current market prices*—the U.S. would be $66 trillion in the hole.[7] Seems problematic. Even Dan Aykroyd got it, on *Saturday Night Live*.

> I will present to Congress the Inflation Maintenance Program, whereby the US Treasury will make up any inflation cost losses through direct tax rebates to the public in cash. Now you may say, "Won't that cost a lot of money? Won't that increase the deficit?" Sure it will, but so what? We'll just print more money.[8]
>
> — Dan Aykroyd, imitating Jimmy Carter, 1978

 **Jeff Bezos** ✓
@JeffBezos   ...

Ouch. Inflation is far too important a problem for the White House to keep making statements like this. It's either straight ahead misdirection or a deep misunderstanding of basic market dynamics.

 **President Biden** ✓ @POTUS   · Jul 2
⚑ United States government official

My message to the companies running gas stations and setting prices at the pump is simple: this is a time of war and global peril.

Bring down the price you are charging at the pump to reflect the cost you're paying for the product. And do it now.

9:42 PM · Jul 2, 2022 · Twitter for iPhone

33.4K Retweets   **7,107** Quote Tweets   **195.9K** Likes

US Oil & Gas Association
@US_OGA   ...

Working on it Mr. President. In the meantime - have a
Happy 4th and please make sure the WH intern who
posted this tweet registers for Econ 101 for the fall
semester...

> **President Biden** ✔ @POTUS · Jul 2
> ⚑ United States government official
>
> My message to the companies running gas stations and setting prices at the
> pump is simple: this is a time of war and global peril.
>
> Bring down the price you are charging at the pump to reflect the cost you're
> paying for the product. And do it now.

10:11 AM · Jul 3, 2022 · Twitter Web App

5,050 Retweets   **535** Quote Tweets   **24.7K** Likes

The answer to the age-old question, "Do rising prices cause inflation or does inflation cause rising prices?" is "Yes."

Inflation is impossible to discuss without introducing gross distortions. The idea that something so complex as the ebb and flow of prices—something akin to global weather patterns—can be described using a binary vocabulary (inflation or deflation) is bonkers. Even if you throw in a few adjectives to smooth the edges, it still doesn't work.

> Now we've had moments in history with extreme leverage, we've had moments in history with extreme inflationary forces, and even speculative environments. But, I assert that we'd never seen these three macro-imbalances occurring all at once.
>
> — Tavi Costa (@TaviCosta) of Crescat Capitol

There is a tribe in Africa that has three numbers: one, two, and many. They were never going to invent calculus. Economists armed with calculus will never be able to describe money flows using only two words. Language corrupts ideas.

Calculating the consumer price index (CPI) requires measuring various consumer prices and then statistically overweighting components that naturally go down (tech) or can't be measured (implicit rent).[9] The Boskin Commission, at the behest of politicians looking to distort the numbers in order to look good and to reduce the cost of inflation-adjusted payouts, came up with a Nobel Prize-worthy concept—the fudge factor. My favorite is "hedonic adjustments." Let's ignore the fact that "hedonic" is defined by some chick named Mirriam Webster as "of, relating to, or characterized by pleasure," whose etymology stems from medieval agricultural economists "choking the chickens."

> For those of you who may be unaware, Boskin is the economist/weasel/fraud who helped to officially distort the CPI, making it more or less worthless as a measure of inflation.
>
> — Barry Ritholtz

Let me illustrate with my favorite example. The blender your grandmother bought in 1945 died after 70 years because you dropped that pig on the floor. It was replaced by a plastic piece of crap with a similar life expectancy to the fruit in your smoothy, and which can't be repaired. The cost per use has soared, as with all the other rapidly depreciating crap in your house, but economists have not yet included accelerated depreciation in the CPI. Thus, the price of the new blender is *not hedonically* adjusted *higher* because it is chintzy; it is hedonically adjusted *lower* because it has more buttons.

Addendum: On December 14, 2022, after completing this diatribe, my blender broke.

Another CPI adjustment is called "substitution." Imagine the price of ribeye has soared from $9/lb to $18/lb (which it has). Economists assume that the savvy shopper will switch to strip steak, which is now way overpriced at $9/lb. Through the miracle of "substitution," Boskinites claim the price of dinner hasn't changed, so there is no inflation. Now switch to neo-Marxist Klaus Schwab's favorite protein—bugs—and we have a deflationary crisis calling for Fed intervention.

The "substitution" correction should be stored alongside the WD40 and duct tape in the pantheon of all-purpose tools. Oddly, economists seem to have overlooked the subtlety that substitution should be hedonically offset by the reduction in quality. Ribeye is twice as expensive because it is twice as good. I propose Collum's Universal Law of Hedonics (CULH):

$$\text{Substitution} \times \text{hedonic} = 1.0.$$

CITY	CY 2015	CY 2016	CY 2017	CY 2018	1ST HALF 2019	LAST HALF 2021–FIRST HALF 2022	AVG
1. New York	10.3%	10.8%	11.2%	12.6%	12.1%	18.44%	11.4%
2. Los Angeles	10.9%	11.1%	11.6%	12.1%	12.6%	18.30%	11.7%
3. Chicago	9.8%	10.9%	11.0%	11.9%	10.7%	18.83%	10.9%
4. Houston	8.4%	8.9%	8.7%	8.8%	9.7%	13.36%	8.9%
5. Philadelphia	10.8%	11.2%	10.8%	10.6%	11.2%	12.84%	10.9%
6. Phoenix	7.6%	8.1%	9.2%	7.4%	7.6%	15.86%	8.0%
7. San Antonio	8.4%	8.8%	8.8%	9.3%	9.8%	16.12%	9.0%
8. San Diego	13.0%	12.2%	11.8%	11.7%	11.2%	18.51%	12.0%
9. Dallas	9.4%	8.9%	9.2%	8.7%	8.4%	16.54%	8.9%
10. San Jose	13.3%	12.9%	13.3%	12.7%	12.6%	18.11%	13.0%

Chapwood Index showing inflation in 10 major cities

Shadowstats.com [10] and the Chapwood Index [11] have both figured out how to determine inflation: they monitor prices without just making shit up. Lo and behold, inflation has been a runaway train for years. However, you must follow the science. Or, as my Maw used to say, "You can like it or lump it." She had other nonsensical aphorisms, such as "TS", which took me years to decipher.

Welp. Choice of metric aside, inflation is finally here. After years of predictions of inflation owing to Fed and government largesse, even the mangled CPI rose by a demonic 8-9 percent. (It's higher for those of us living in reality.)

Dave Collum
@DavidBCollum

My brother, a former accountant, keeps track of everything. Year-over-year his food bill is up 41%.

11:49 AM · Jul 26, 2022 · Twitter Web App

ılı View Tweet analytics

3,102 Retweets   **195** Quote Tweets   **16.5K** Likes

Notice the number of likes on that otherwise sterile tweet. I hit a nerve that day. Another accountant replied, concurring that he gets the same number. Jim Iuorio of CNBC fame says his restaurant—yes, an Italian restaurant—is seeing 25 percent hikes in food costs.

Entering an inflationary period while entering an economic recession hits two other hot bones that have crawled up my ass. Who defined a recession as a period in which an economy turns down? According to Mirriam of Mensa, a recession is "the act or action of receding." OK, I gotta let that one go, but I should add that they don't want to use the word "depression" because Mirriam calls that "a place or part that is lower than the surrounding area."

Thus, to exit a recession you need only to turn upward (moving off the first derivative of zero). Exiting a depression is like exiting a sand trap: you must exit the other side. Golfers spending time in sand traps surely understand depressions.

My second bone to pick is that boomers will recall from their childhoods that economists believed that stagnation and inflation could not co-exist, forcing them to invent a new word, "stagflation." Think about this: economists were shocked that consumers buying fewer goods and services with the same amount of income put a drag on the economy. I should have become an economist—a low bar to clear—but that would have required me to take at least one course in economics.

> Aside from priorities, is this even true? Is there any good reason to believe that inflation hits low-income households especially hard?
>
> — Paul Krugman (@paulkrugman), former economist

> I think nobody thought about logistic supply chains or any of that stuff until suddenly it became a big problem.
>
> — Paul Krugman, utterly clueless

For years, Twitter was littered with people ranting about how inflation would chip away at their debt. How is that working for you? Is that mortgage payment shrinking, or even getting easier to pay?

What these inflationary virgins did not understand is that wages can be very sticky, whether owing to multi-year contracts or just psychology. Over 70 percent of Americans say their paycheck is not keeping pace with expenses.[12] The other 30 percent don't have a paycheck.

In 2019 the so-called median deplorable earned $60,000 but couldn't find $400 to replace their rapidly depreciating appliance without turning to credit. They now are ranting, since that $6,000 reduction in real spending power will leave a scar.

They've also discovered that only a little of their monthly budget is discretionary. You can't cut back on your tax bill; mine will increase by eight percent in each of the next two years, according to inside sources. That microchip-rich car can't be fixed in your garage, and it ain't gonna fix itself. You can cut those violin lessons—the little rug rat sucked anyway—but the hockey is non-negotiable.

That mortgage hasn't changed, but the escrowed taxes, insurance, and maintenance costs sure have. It also looks like you may have overpaid for that shack, making your abode and your 401K the only deflation in your personal universe.

> There is a great deal of Americans where it is uncomfortable that they're spending more, but they are not gonna go under. You've got to stop complaining ... you still have your job ... so I'm gonna need you to calm down and back off.[13]
>
> — MSNBC guest

PERSONAL FINANCE

With higher inflation, living with your parents makes economic sense

Let's stop joking about young adults living in their parents' basement. Financial independence doesn't have to come with a monthly rent payment.

Perspective by Michelle Singletary
Columnist
Yesterday at 7:00 a.m. EDT

Let me drive this point home, using inflation to illustrate the miracle of compounding in reverse. Every year we all get some kind of raise (or not). During the Great Financial Crisis, or GFC, Cornell University announced there would be no raises that year. On a campus with a faculty brandishing an estimated 2.5 million total SAT points, three business schools, and countless on-the-spectrum math geniuses wandering around in a daze, nobody seemed to notice that we got pegged. That three or four percent of lost salary persists year after year until you retire, amounting to an entire annual salary lost if you are young.

Inflation whacked us this year, too: 3.5 percent raises into the teeth of eight percent inflation reduced our salaries by another few percentage points. Now we are talking about a reduction of over eight percent in our lifetime earnings in just two bad years.

I'm an old guy, and the compounding of my annual salary movements is nearly over. I will top off the tank by staying on payroll, wandering the halls babbling incoherently, and occasionally soiling myself (SNAFU).

> One original thought is worth 1,000 meaningless quotes.
>
> — Banksy

I got into an argument with David Andolfatto of the St. Louis Fed years back, in which he asserted that Fed chairman Paul Volcker *contributed* to inflation. Sounds like he was making an odd case, but those interest rates were ramming returns of over 15 percent into the banking system and consumers' pockets. Maybe Volcker's recession initiated the reversal of the inflation mindset and money flows, while

Russia's cheap resources, China's cheap labor, and the U.S.'s great demographics did the heavy lifting. A decade later, I'm still pondering Andolfatto's thesis.

> Engineering a higher nominal GDP growth through a higher structural level of inflation is a proven way to get rid of high levels of debt. That's exactly how many countries, including the US and the UK, got rid of their debt after World War II.[14]
>
> — Russell Napier, author of *Anatomy of a Bear*

> There is too much debt in the world, so they must inflate it away, which they will. That's the only thing you need to know.[15]
>
> — Eric Peters, CIO of One River Asset Management

Ominously, the inflation is global.[16] How else could the dollar be so strong in the forex markets? Germany, for example, put together back-to-back quarters of 33 percent rises in producer prices (45 percent year-over-year in September 2022), which ought to scare the hell out of all of us, given their history.[17]

The combined balance sheets of the world's central banks has grown tenfold in less than two decades.[18] We have a global debt problem which appears to be getting addressed by global inflation.

Much of it comes from the tens of trillions of dollars rammed into the global system during and following the GFC,[19,20] and then trillions more to enable the IFL (Insane Fucking Lockdown) that completely screwed up the supply chains. If the Fed had not promised somebody behind closed doors that they would do their part, the lockdown would not have happened. No Fed, no lockdown. Now you know who to blame.

Inflation Rate in European Union increased to 11.50 percent in October from 10.90 percent in September of 2022. source: EUROSTAT

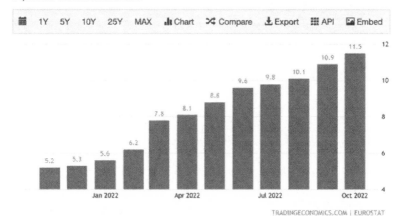

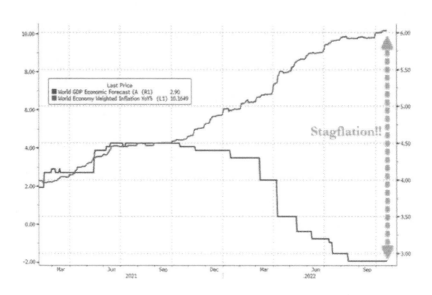

Let's not allow that "inflate away debt" idea—Ray Dalio's "beautiful deleveraging"—to go uncontested. It reminds me of picking yourself up by your bootstraps; have you ever tried to do it? Those who say the world is doing it right now seem unaware that the rate of debt growth is outpacing inflation. Hard to see how that gets you anywhere. The U.S. debt-to-GDP ratio has grown by over 15 percent in four years.[21]

Jesse Felder
@jessefelder   ...

"Inflation is a very serious subject. You can argue it's the way democracies die. It's a huge danger... If you overdo it too much, you ruin your civilization."

cnbc.com

Wobbling on a weak understanding of global finance, I called out to fintwit for examples of countries that inflated away their debt *without a deflationary default in the end.* (Of course, inflation is a default too, but humor me.) I got answers, many from smart guys who thought their answers were obvious but which don't work for me.

- Weimar Germany? No. They screwed the populace but big sovereign debts were denominated in gold, ultimately leading to WWII.
- Argentina? *Please.* They defaulted six times in the last century.
- An obscure answer: Canada in the 1980s and 1990s? They did burn down their debt, but the inflation rate was way too low to account for it; austerity and growth get a lot of the credit.
- Japan? Nope. Although not imploding yet, their debt-to-GDP ratio is a monster, with inflation just beginning to flicker.

The post-WW II United States for the win! It had double-digit negative rates on sovereign debt, and bondholders were crushed. So that is a valid case, but let us not forget that the U.S. was the only industrial nation standing—a juggernaut, controlling 80 percent of global GDP. How much post-war debt reduction was inflation and how much was American Exceptionalism (a term coined by Stalin)? Someone smarter than me could do that math.

> The Russian invasion of Ukraine has put an end to the globalization we have experienced over the last three decades. A large-scale reorientation of supply chains will inherently be inflationary.
>
> — Larry Fink, CEO of Blackrock

There are other ominous problems looming. The world is said to be at the precipice of deglobalizing, propelled by a collapse of the global population. Yes, you heard that right. Imploding. Deglobalization means that goods and services may no longer be made most efficiently and economically. Peter Zeihan claims that population collapse and accompanying deglobalization are already baked into the cake.[22]

The conflict in Ukraine has been horrible for inflation since energy prices drive the prices of everything, and one could imagine the conflict accelerating deglobalization. If the conflict worsens or spreads, I'd say it is time to panic.

> I grew up in France, so I had a good dose of Marx in my education. The first thing Marx teaches you is that revolutions are typically the result of inflation.
>
> — Louis-Vincent Gave, 2021

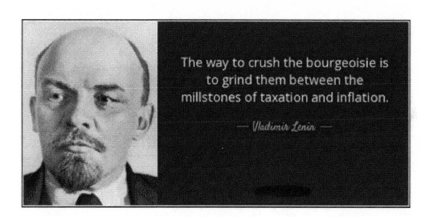

THE FED

> We have got to get inflation behind us. I wish there were a painless way to do that, there isn't ... there will be pain.
>
> — Jerome "J-Pain" Powell, being clear

> We're going to have a good deal of pain and suffering before we can solve these things.
>
> — William McChesney Martin, 1969 (and there *was* pain to come)

THE FEDERAL RESERVE BANK is now in a bind. The drag queen shows at the Eccles Building are over. Forty years of disinflation and jawboning to the point of blowers' cramp created a gargantuan recency bias, leaving generations of Americans unfamiliar with the socioeconomic horrors that bad monetary policy can inflict on an economy and society. We are confronting an inflation problem, but what policy tools do we have to defeat it?

Recall that when Volcker took on the inflation Balrog, the U.S. national debt was 31 percent of GDP. Now it is more than four times that. Total public and private debt relative to GDP is up almost threefold. Volcker did not have to worry about the systemic risk that his successors at the Fed nurtured to maturity. Since the Fed has been accused of keeping rates "too low for too long" too many times by too many smart guys, they can't plead ignorance no matter how compelling that defense seems.

> Hiking rates to bring down inflation is not a "policy mistake," it's the Fed's mandate. The true policy mistake was believing that 0% rates, buying billions of mortgage bonds in a housing bubble, & increasing the money supply by 40% in 2 yrs would have no negative consequences.
>
> — Charlie Biello, CEO of Compound Capital Advisors

Leading up to 2019, the Fed belatedly started raising interest rates and reducing its balance sheet. I thought it was *way* too late, and possibly a mistake to do them concurrently.

The repo market started convulsing in late 2019, prompting the Fed to pivot yet again by "going direct"—shoving money straight at the consumers—at the behest of a Blackrock white paper.[1,2,3] A few months later the Fed agreed to put the economy in an induced COVID coma, causing much bigger problems.

Inflation is now in our DNA as the dreaded "inflation expectations" have taken root. Unlike his predecessors, Powell is in a brawl with fiscal policymakers—way too many tools inside the beltway, spending money to slay inflation—over whom he has no control and with whom he has no allegiance.

> It will turn out to be largely impossible to normalize interest rates without collapsing the economy.
>
> — Edward Chancellor, market historian

The second fundamental problem is one of legacy and credibility. Many market participants—pivot watchers—see Powell *et al.* as swamp creatures, controlled by some higher power to mitigate all pain and damage. I see him as a guy who wants to enter the pantheon of central bankers alongside Paul Volcker, but who is being compared with the profoundly destructive Arthur Burns by the likes of Roach, Summers, and others.[4,5] Bill Gross called them an "ignorant—yes ignorant— Federal Reserve" while making allusions to "Ponzi finance."[6]

Which path will a narcissist at the peak of his power choose: protector of credibility and legacy, or savior of markets and destroyer of currencies? I suspect legacy wins, but it is just a hunch. The markets are currently taking the other side of the bet.

> So far, Jerome Powell looks more like Arthur Burns than Paul Volcker.
>
> — Bill Dudley, former head of the New York Federal Reserve

Before looking at what the Fed might do, and with what level of fortitude, let's look at what prominent Fed detractors have to say, juxtaposed with a few Fed comments for comic relief. Mind you, most of these are not just loose-cannon bloggers.

> The country is suffering from the worst cost-of-living crisis in 42 years. The Fed wasn't data-dependent and now has sacrificed its credibility.
>
> — Lacy Hunt, Hoisington Investment Management and former deflationist

This is the fundamental problem ... It is a fundamental trap ... It's gonna be really bad. I think we should worry more about deflation. I think that is a huge risk people aren't thinking about. If the Fed pops this bubble there will be a deflationary spiral ... It is going to cause devastation.[7]

— Mark Spitznagel, Universa Investments, on Dr. Frankenstein and the monster

There is a whole generation of people who don't remember inflation. They don't know what it is, and so I think inflation is a non-existent threat.

— Alice Rivlin, former Fed governor, circa 2017

The Fed's latest moves are consistent with a central bank that is continuously scrambling to catch up with realities on the ground. It is the kind of thing that one typically finds in developing countries with weak institutions, not in the issuer of the world's reserve currency and the custodian of the world's most sophisticated financial markets.

— Mohamed El-Erian, former CEO of PIMCO

Their job is to fight inflation. They've done a terrible job of it so far.

— Jeff Gundlach, founder of Doubleline Capital, in reference to the Fed

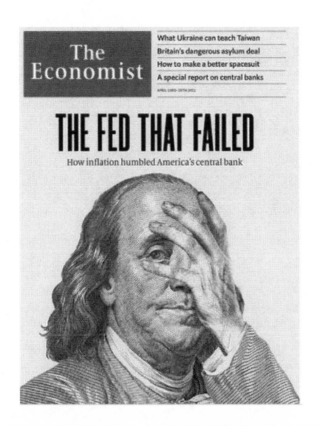

The Economist

What Ukraine can teach Taiwan
Britain's dangerous asylum deal
How to make a better spacesuit
A special report on central banks

APRIL 23RD–29TH 2022

THE FED THAT FAILED

How inflation humbled America's central bank

I think we're in one of those very difficult periods where simply capital preservation is I think the most important thing we can strive for ... [The Fed] has inflation on the one hand, slowing growth on the other, and they're going to be clashing all the time. You can't think of a worse environment than where we are right now for financial assets ... Look at the level of overvaluation we're in right now in terms of rates and stocks ... Sub-two-percent inflation is a much better problem to have than above-two-percent inflation.[8]

— Paul Tudor Jones of Tudor Investment Corp.

Hitting or exceeding 2 percent inflation for a few months does not mean victory. To fully achieve the goal of price stability, we need to see a sustained period of moderately above-target inflation. Only then will the job be complete.[9]

— Mary Daly, San Francisco Fed President, in 2020, showing *zero* understanding of "price stability"

I don't feel the pain of inflation anymore. I see prices rising but I have enough ... I sometimes balk at the price of things, but I don't find myself in a space where I have to make tradeoffs because I have enough, and many Americans have enough.[10]

— Mary Daly in 2022, showing *zero* understanding of inflation

I know from studying history that credit eventually kills all great societies. We have essentially taken out our American Express card and said we are going to have a great time ... Perhaps we are simply responding to the same type of cycles that most advanced civilizations fell prey to, whether it was the Romans, sixteenth-century Spain, eighteenth-century France, or nineteenth-century Britain.[11]

— Paul Tudor Jones

The West is now awakening from decades of poor policy. The consequences will appear overwhelming at first. We'll get through, but that long, painful process has only just begun.[12]

— Eric Peters, CIO of One River Asset Management

I think now we have more credibility, we're moving faster, we will be able to bring inflation under control sooner and with less disruption to the economy than we had in the '70s.

— James Bullard, President of the St. Louis Fed

The Fed's application of its framework has left it behind the curve in controlling inflation. This, in turn, has made a hard landing virtually inevitable.

— Bill Dudley

Because inflation is ultimately a monetary phenomenon, the Federal Reserve has the capacity and the responsibility to ensure inflation expectations are firmly anchored at—and not below—our target.

— Lael Brainard, current vice chair of the Federal Reserve, May 16, 2019

Staff economists at the Federal Reserve predict ... a measured inflation rate of slightly less than 2% in 2022, according to minutes of the September Federal Open Market Committee meeting released last Wednesday.

— James Grant, @Grantspub, October 2021

Valuations have only begun to retreat from record extremes as a decline in the economy begins and at a time when the Fed is not only unable to come to its rescue but is forced to implement policy that will only make things worse.

— Jesse Felder, The Felder Report

The length of predicted recession—two full years—is extraordinary. Add to that probably the most bearish comment I have ever heard from a Fed bank—"the odds of a hard landing are around 80%" and wow!

— Albert Edwards, Societe General (SocGen)

We want to see inflation move up to 2%. And we mean that on a sustainable basis. We don't mean just tap the brakes once. But then we'd also like to see it on track to move moderately above 2% for some time.

— Jerome Powell, April 2021, on pain avoidance

Possibly the most robust indicator of an impending recession is when the Fed dismisses the inverting yield curve as a predictor of an impending recession.

— Albert Edwards

You know what upsets me the most? People say why do you get so exercised about the Federal Reserve? It's because the people they screwed going in were the lower and middle-class people, and the people getting screwed on the way out are those same people. They're getting it on both ends.

— Guy Adami, money manager and CNBC host (a good one)

The Fed doesn't want to get into the credit allocation business.

— Loretta Mester, Cleveland Fed president, after buying $1.3 trillion of mortgage-backed securities in less than two years

It could be useful to be able to intervene directly in assets where the prices have a more direct link to spending decisions.

— Janet "Yeltsin" Yellen, on credit allocation

The Fed since Volcker has been pretty clueless and remains so. What has been more remarkable, though, is the persistent confidence ... despite the demonstrable ineptness in dealing with asset bubbles.

— Jeremy Grantham, founder of GMO

Now that the Fed finds itself in such an uncomfortable situation—one largely of its own making—it may be inclined to eschew further rate hikes, particularly given the growing criticism that it is tipping the economy into recession, destroying wealth, and fueling instability. Yet such a course of action would risk repeating the monetary-policy mistake of the 1970s, saddling America and the world with an even longer period of stagflationary trends.

— Mohamed El-Erian

We are on the cusp of a rare paradigm shift in interest rates. Such changes take decades—or even generations—to occur. But when they do, the financial implications are profound.

— Nick Giambruno of *The Financial Underground*

Since 2010, Central Bankers became active market participants—uneconomic market participants with infinite balance sheets, seeking to distort market mechanisms for pricing of risk. These distortions spread into all financial markets ... this easing cycle has no precedent and undoing something so unique will not resemble previous cycles ... To return balance sheets to where they were in 2010 at the beginning of QE would mean a sale of $20 trillion in assets, or roughly equivalent to selling the entire $24 trillion in U.S. annual GDP.[13]

— Lindsay Politi, One River Asset Management

Underlying inflation appears to still be well anchored at levels consistent with the Fed's average 2 percent objective, and so—unlike in the Volker and Greenspan eras—no extra monetary restraint is needed to bring trend inflation down.[14]

— Charles Evans, president of the Chicago Fed

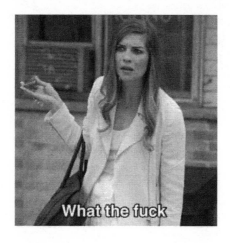

> We will not allow inflation to rise above 2% or less ... We could raise interest rates in 15 minutes if we had to.
>
> — Ben Bernanke, winner of the 2022 Nobel Prize in Economics

> Thank you, President Fisher, I know we put a lot of value on anecdotal reports around this table, and often to great credit. But I do want to urge you not to overweight the macroeconomic opinions of private-sector people who are not trained in economics.
>
> — Ben Bernanke

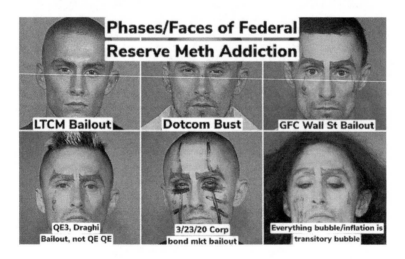

The Fed's bad policy flipped the last of the hard core deflationists—Napier, Hunt, and Shedlock—to call for serious inflation; David Rosenberg thinks so.[15]

I am going to disagree with Milton Friedman here: I did not believe inflation is just a monetary problem or government spending problem. It may start that way, but it mutates. Now the Fed has to deal with the Bronteroc. By assuming inflation is always just a monetary phenomenon, market participants stop thinking, because the Fed has their backs. I think this model is now wrong.

> I think the Fed absolutely does not get the pain associated with a collapsing bubble.[16]
>
> — Jeremy Grantham

I am not sure there is widespread agreement on the Fed's goals. Is it to fight inflation, pop an all-time record bubble across all asset classes, euthanize the market zombies,[17,18] regain credibility by detonating the Fed put[19] (the implicit guarantee under the markets), or ... wait for it ... destroy the Europeans?[20] Maybe Powell is channeling the legendary King Canute, showing that even the most omnipotent king can't stem the tides.

No matter what, the bulk of the stock toshers seem unwilling to grasp that the Fed will push rates up until the will to speculate is broken. Michael Every of Rabobank suggests "They are being told clearly they can no longer have their cake, and everyone else's cake, and eat it and fit in their jeans. And they are ignoring it."[21]

> Failure is not an option for Jay Powell. I think they're going to 4% come hell or high water. Until inflation comes down a lot, the Fed is really a single-mandate central bank.[22]
>
> — Richard Clarida, former Fed vice chair

Does the Fed have the fortitude? The Bank of England folded fast to save their pension system.[23] Some thought the Fed couldn't lift rates above one percent.[24] This is no longer "four-teen days to flatten the yield curve." They are up against a wall.

- "The Fed has never before started a rate hiking cycle when inflation was already 7.9%." [25]
- An anonymous (but prominent) commentator with the pseudonym of Mr. Skin noted how many times Powell has referred to "real interest rates" and said he wanted them "over +1%." They are at about –10% right now, so that is an unveiled threat to "unwind unknown globs of leverage."
- Roach sees the "Fed funds rate up 10% from here." [26] Powell insisted that a neutral policy stance is "not a place to pause or stop" and that the Fed would embrace "a restrictive policy stance for some time."
- Fed President Loretta Mester warned that they would raise rates "even in a recession."

I don't think the Fed is gonna let up just because the economy starts popping a few rivets. There isn't enough blood in the streets for a Theranos lab test. Before this is over, there will be bloated corpses, shattered dreams, and milk cartons with Cathie Wood's face.

> I am still waiting for [Powell] to act boldly—"boldly" means he has to shock the market. If you want to change someone's view, if you want to change someone's action, you can't slap them on the hand, you have to hit them in the face.
>
> — Henry Kauffman, legend

> The Federal Reserve appears to be braced and wants participants in the market to understand they will stay the course ... the rough landing odds are very high ... Monetary policy is currently on the right course but current right course will have to persevere.
>
> — Lacy Hunt

What about other central banks? It appears they have been cast adrift while we try to solve our domestic problems. This could become a monetary Monroe Doctrine. The strengthening dollar is wreaking havoc on global credit markets. The Fed sent a few currency swaps to alleviate a few currencies being pegged by the strong dollar, but my sympathies are not high. We have a derivatives market of $2 quadrillion notional value that has overstayed its welcome in the world of wealth creation, serving only to finance finance. The Swiss National Bank stress really leaves me cold, since they were printing francs to buy U.S. equities. When in Econ 101 did you guys learn about that? Fuck 'em.

"THE CENTRAL BANK DOES TAKE ACCOUNT OF THE IMPACT ITS POLICIES HAVE ON THE REST OF THE WORLD BUT WOULD CONTINUE TO LIFT INTEREST RATES TO BRING INFLATION UNDER CONTROL."

— FED CHAIR JEROME POWELL, IN RESPONSE TO THE U.N WARNING FURTHER RATE HIKES WOULD CAUSE FURTHER PAIN IN EMERGING MARKETS

We now understand better how little we understand about inflation.

—Jerome Powell

BROKEN MARKETS

> My money remains on the likelihood that this is the
> early stages of a profound bear market in assets.
> Populism in the west has a long way to go. QE has
> undermined savings, and now populism will
> undermine the price mechanism. We are at the
> start of a 25-year cycle, so get used to it.
>
> — Crispin Odey, Odey Asset Management and a
> notorious bear

I SUSPECT THAT the broken Year in Review clock is finally
right. What we will find out is whether it blows up your house at
high noon. The presumption that bailouts by the Fed would
always be forthcoming and would always work has enabled
investors to buy speculative non-GAAP tech garbage. That
model may be tested.

We are looking at some events that have not been seen for
many years (decades). For starters, we are coming off a frothy
high in the equity markets, said to be the biggest bubble of
them all. This is occurring concurrently with a serious, if not
potentially disastrous, downturn in the bond market.

Recall that a 60:40 portfolio in the 2007–09 bear market
was cushioned by the bond market. The risk parity cult—those
striving to bring the risks and rewards of stocks and bonds to
parity by leveraging their bond portfolios—may have overshot
their mark. We also haven't seen inflation levels like this for
four decades.

To top it off, we are not coming off a euphoric high. Investors may have done well in their portfolios, but all other geopolitical and social pressures have left us plebes in sour moods. Entering a secular bear market in stocks and bonds pissed off at the world is not a solid foundation for a long slog.

> When I look back at the bull market that we've had in financial assets really starting in 1982. All the factors that created that boom not only have stopped, they've reversed ... We are in deep trouble.
>
> — Stan Druckenmiller

A Fed boxed in by rapidly rising but still historically low interest rates and serious inflation is akin to a visit to your oncologist. What comes next? You get your affairs in order.

The luminary Murray Stahl of Horizon Kinetics has a way with words. He notes that "the Age of Monetary Policy is over." Channeling some of Murray's thoughts, blended with a few of my own, we may be at the end of a unique economic cycle.

In the early 1980s the Russians were starved of capital and began flooding the world with dirt-cheap commodities. The Chinese were also starved of capital—quite literally, China had $38,000 of foreign reserves in its banking system as it exited its self-exile [1]— and began flooding the market with dirt-cheap labor. U.S. long bond rates began a four-decade trek from 16 percent to about zero. Meanwhile, the boomer demographic not only hit the workforce, but brought their wives with them, in large numbers.

I have argued generously that buybacks are a reach for yield, given the low returns even on fortress balance sheets, but debt-fueled price pumping nicely propelled executive stock option valuations too.

These tailwinds will not repeat over the next four decades. Globalization is fraying at the edges and, according to Zeihan, will be ripped apart in a global demographic collapse.[2]

> Prior droughts have been due to rising inflation and/or high market valuation. The U.S. is now at risk from both ... U.S. returns are at now risk from both the prospect of higher inflation AND the headwind to returns from high starting-point valuations.
>
> — Gerard Minack, Minack Advisors and former Morgan Stanley economist

> A simple reversion to trend, if it happened tomorrow, would require the S&P 500 Index to fall back below 2,000, the prospect of an even greater decline is a frightening one, indeed.
>
> — Jesse Felder, The Felder Report

And, by the way, my definition of a correction is that it adjusts asset values *and* investors' attitudes *significantly*. When was our last correction? March 2020? Not a chance. What attitudes were corrected? How about 2007–09? Not in my book. Investors were rewarded for their tenacity.

The last real correction was 1967–81. Equity investors lost 70 percent of their equity gains, inflation corrected. You could not give equities away even though, by all metrics, they were dirt cheap. Why take a risk on equities after 14 years of bludgeoning?

Every year I take a swipe at valuations. Two years ago I went at the egregiously overpriced FAANGs and related tech garbage. Moreover, the FAANGs *et al.* have an enormous collective market cap compared to the dot-coms that caused pain.[3] Although the FAANGs *et al.* humiliated me in 2021 by continuing their moonshot, their two-year returns are slightly sobering and exonerating.

Two-year total returns of the FAANGs *et al.* critiqued in 2020

- Amazon   −43%
- Apple   +9%
- Facebook *   −56%
- Genius Brands   −59%
- Google   +7%
- Microsoft   +6%
- Netflix   −46%
- Nvidia   +26%
- Salesforce   −31%
- Shopify   −62%
- Tesla   −30%
- Zoom   −81%

* Metaverse

Today, only finance is profitable, while production is in crisis.

— Thierry Meyssan, French journalist

At the end of 2021, an analysis of 25 valuation metrics showed the markets to be 120–150 percent above historical fair value.[4,5] I *obsessed* over 1994 as the year when valuations left the Earth's gravitational field. The markets have been steadily climbing the wall of worry since then, residing above historic fair value, with occasional pauses that refresh, propelled by (a) a bond rout intervention in 1994 that never really stopped, and (b) the rapid rise of passive index investing.

The curve below has no mathematical basis, but I think it captures the problem and the 1994 launch date nicely.

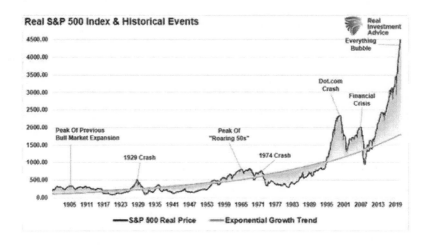

Real S&P 500 Index & Historical Events

Find a metric that makes you more optimistic—be my guest—but it would be perilous to ignore the 25 I laid out in detail last year.[6] With the S&P executing an orderly swan dive of 20 percent as of December 16, 2022, many investors are looking to buy the dips. Do you really think the unwinding of less than two years of froth is all we are going to get? If I had told you two years ago that you wouldn't make *any* gains through 2022, would you have soiled your adult diapers? Of course not.

It is not time to yell, "Cut me." It is time to pull out James Stack's 2013 chart showing what the Bear does to the Bull.

Alas, the removal of such froth is merely phase one of a secular bear market. Phase two rides in on the back of the recession, accompanied by lost revenues, mean reversion of what are currently record profit margins, and the disappearance of credit-constrained share buybacks. Phase three is when the blood, cadavers, broken bones, and shattered teeth litter the

Street. Only then have we reached the Charles Manson helter-skelter market. The rotting corpses of malinvestments—the Enrons, Tycos, Worldcoms, Lehmans, and heaven knows how many banks—will be stinking up the joint.

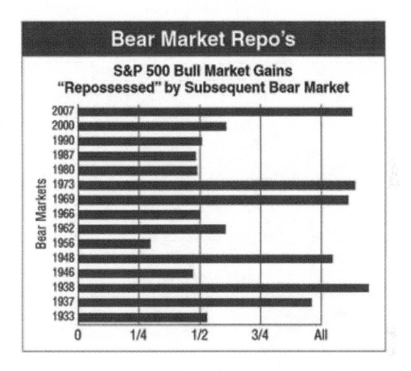

Images of the 1921 Russian famine come to mind. In his 2022 book, *The Price of Time*, Edward Chancellor reminds us that, without exception, whenever rates have been artificially suppressed, the story has ended in tragedy—*every single time.*

Markets are up 26% in six months.

— Nikkei Bulls, January 1, 1991

Contrary to lessons learned from Greenspan, Bernanke, Yellen, Powell, and "Whatever-It-Takes" Draghi, the markets can be uninvestable. Take the Nikkei. If you were in it in 1989 your capital gains are still underwater, even *without* correcting for inflation. It took over 30 years to get above the '89 high on a total return basis (including dividends but not fees, taxes, and inflation).[7] If you weren't in it then but averaged down *starting* in 1989, it took you two decades to break even.

Just when you think it can't get any worse

...Along comes someone to prove you wrong

As the guest speaker in one of George Nobel's Twitter spaces, I argued the Nikkei was uninvestable.[8] The quick counter was that you short it. First, shorting is speculating, not investing. Second, you would be slaughtered because it took too long. The U.S. markets in 1967–81 were also widow makers.

Speculation is a zero-sum game in which speculators vie with each other for profits that they, in the aggregate, cannot achieve.

— T. A. Hieronymus, University of Illinois professor of Agricultural Economics

It is time for speculators to refresh their memories that two and two add up to four, not eight or ten.[9]

— *Time* magazine, 1967

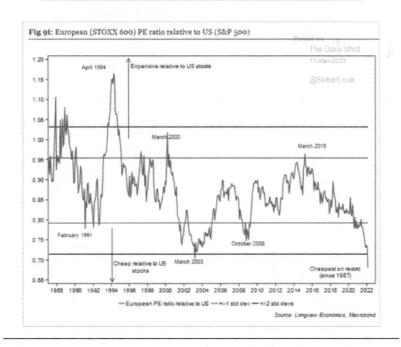

Fig 91: European (STOXX 600) PE ratio relative to US (S&P 500)

The big European markets, including the DAX, FTSE, and CAC, have been treading water off their highs of more than two decades ago. Maybe they are finally cheap, but be careful about grading on a curve.

When Murray Stahl says that the age of monetary policy is over, a corollary might be that the Age of the V-Bounce is over. If I am right, buying opportunities will be followed by even better ones for a very long time. Headline-grabbing crashes do not correct investor attitudes; attitudes are corrected by markets grinding investors to dust over *years*. Somebody will make money—Taleb's *Fooled by Randomness* says this—but it's unlikely to be you or me.

I believe we are in the biggest bear market in my life. This is just the second inning. A lot more to come ... There's no other country on earth that has staked so much of its net wealth in stocks. But we are at a very big peak of complacency.[10]

— David Wright, 78-year-old co-founder of Sierra Investment Management

Warren "Never Bet Against America" Buffett noted that most of the top 20 companies in the world 30 years ago were Japanese, and that no Japanese companies are in the top six today.[11] He then asks rhetorically if you have figured out which will be the next top 20 and, implicitly, in which continent they will be domiciled.

On an upbeat note, Felder says "valuations of U.S. large-cap value stocks relative to growth stocks are now 2.8 standard deviations cheaper than the long-term mean." First, that is relative to growth stocks, and as Hussman has noted repeatedly, The Bear eats anything and everything. All valuation deciles drop. A P/E ratio of 10 might sound cheap, but there is no immutable law of markets that says it can't drop to five.

Over the last 40 years the capital gain on the S&P grew about six percent annualized (inflation-corrected but not including dividends, taxes, and fees, which are nearly self-canceling).

Meanwhile, U.S. GDP grew 3.5 percent annually (including an implicit inflation correction). Greater than three percent—half of those annualized gains—are valuation expansions. Can we extend that potentially mean-regressing disparity over the next 40 years?

Flip the argument and ponder what happens if we *lose* 3.5 percent annually for the next 40 years, owing to contracting valuations. You make nothing but dividends, minus fees and tax-loss writeoffs. You will make nothing.

I will *yet again* post this following chart from Ron Griess (The Chart Store) with blue lines brought to you by ChemDraw. Those blue lines represent 40–75 years of treading water off of market tops. There is a shot clock in basketball but not in investing.

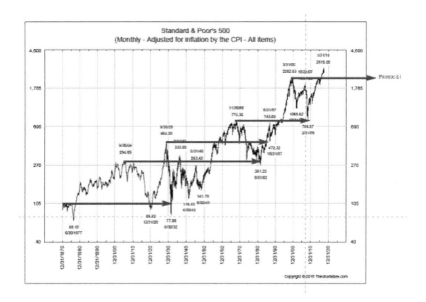

On the next page is another repeated chart.

With few exceptions, charts showing market performance without inflation corrections are misleading if not worthless. You can mentally adjust for inflation using the Rule of 72,[12] but why can't analysts just do it as a courtesy? Since the CPI has long since gone into disrepute, how do you correct for inflation when nobody believes the numbers?

This plot, which I also got from Ron Griess (and can find nowhere else), shows the S&P market performance versus the M2 money supply, which was readily available until the Fed stopped reporting it a few years ago.

Very odd. Is it possible that we have witnessed *zero* real capital gains over the most fabulous century in history? Are dividends (minus fees and taxes) your only source of real gain? But dividends are half what they were in the first half of the twentieth century! Indeed, that is consistent with my conclusion that equity markets are 100 percent overvalued. It's arithmetic.

S&P Composite and Adjusted S&P Composite
(Monthly High/Low Adjusted by M2 Money Supply Growth)

We find it interesting to see that the "real" S&P price has never taken out the 1929 high when one adjusts the S&P by the growth of M2 money supply. We also find it interesting how many times the horizontal trend line has been touched.

Data as of June, 2022

Copyright © 2022 Thechartstore.com

I think that we've had 15 years of Disneyland that has destroyed the economic structure. Think about it: no interest rates. So anyone who's today 40 years old has no experience in markets. Zero. They don't know what time-value of money is.

— Nassim Taleb, September 15, 2022

That's my best shot at euthanizing your hopes and dreams. Before covering a couple more topics, let's pause to "bullet" a few nuggets that crossed my path.

- Bank of America announced zero down payment, zero closing cost mortgages for Black and Hispanic first-time homebuyers [13] in its new Tuskegee Mortgage Program.
- Overpayment for cars during the lockdown will likely cause a car variant of jingle mail as the prices drop well below the

loan value. The loans during the lockdown were ultra-loose, but banks are now shrinking the loan durations as default risks rise. The big **PPP** loans were used to buy Lamborghinis; strategic defaults and repos are spiking.[14]

- The municipal pension funds are still grossly underfunded, gutting their budgets and using leverage to keep up, turning cities into shitholes.

- According to a Blackrock exec, **ERISA** rules say that your fiduciary responsibility precludes overlaying social agendas.[15] The ESG craze was ill-advised *and* illegal. Well, there was too much money to be made by pushing ESG governance into industries and asset classes, so the authorities fixed that.[16] It remains ill-advised.

- The chief financial officer of troubled Blood Bath and Beyond (**BBY**) jumped to his death.[17] The ultimate insult would be a posthumous boost in the share price, but it remains 96 percent off its all-time high. (I thought about buying **BBY** years ago but dodged that bullet.)

- Pension expert Ted Seidle says the state pension underfunding is without precedent, and is not caused by low contributions or low returns but rather mismanagement and corruption by Wall Street (overcharging). Seidle has personally raked in over $100 million on whistleblower awards while boomers slip into poverty.[18]

- Robinhood, the brokerage firm of meme stock investors, is 80 percent off its 2021 **IPO** price. The whole thing was a scam.

- Wisdom Tree's 3x short nickel fund blew up. Some speculators were wiped out as nickel rose 250 percent in two days, triggered by the Rooskies in Ukraine.[19] Chinese nickel titan Tsingshan Holding Group had the same problem but was bailed out by **JPM**, for reasons unknown to me.[20] The exchange just canceled the losing trades. The big guys seldom lose. Hedge fund Elliot Associates is scrambling in the courts to get back $500 million of negated trades.[21]

- Good news: The SPAC craze—funds with cash but no ideas, akin to the South Sea Bubble—seems to be waning, as are non-fungible tokens (NFTs), which are basically autographed images from the internet.

Wall Street Silver ✔ @WallStreetSilv · 12h
Logan Paul paid $623,000 for this NFT that's now worth $10 ......

Draw your own conclusions ...

an NFT I bought for $623,000 that's now worth $10

   567   621   4,644

- SNAP—the most onomatopoeic stock in the markets—dropped 88 percent from its 2021 high, placing it uncomfortably below its 2017 IPO price.
- European banks appear to be in serious trouble, with Credit Suisse and Deutsche Bank (DB) trading at $3 and

$10, respectively. DB is off 92 percent stretched over 26 years—*26 years.* CS is off only 78 percent over that same period but is down 94 percent from its 2007 high.

- Cathie Wood is still in the game, and still hawking her wares on CNBC.

With rates on the rise, GAAP earnings on the decline, and the global economy flirting with recession, the walking dead will be roaming until they run out of credit.

There is no formal definition of a zombie company, but according to economists at the Federal Reserve, they are "companies that have too fucking much debt and pathetic earnings that can't pay the interest on their loans without taking on more debt or doing handjobs behind the dumpster at Wendy's." [23] In short, their cash flows don't cover their interest payments.

Luminaries claim that 20-40 percent of the S&P 500 are zombies. That's 100-200 destitute megacompanies. More optimistic estimates assert that only 20 percent of the Russell 2000 are in the zombie spiral, which surely should have a higher percentage than the S&P since they are mostly story stocks.

I have had no luck locating a list of the S&P 500 zombies.[24] Stephanie Pomboy reminded me that it is a moving target. It does not require a vivid imagination to believe that they are proliferating in a rising interest rate environment. There will be plenty of debt-for-equity swaps (liquidations) as distressed asset investors pick at the carcasses.

> Prepare to see an absolute ONSLAUGHT of corp defaults and downgrades. The myth of corp B/S strength is about to be shattered spectacularly.
>
> — Stephanie Pomboy, 90 percent invested in precious metals (excluding house and cash)

In response to a podcast in which I begged for help, a woman named Alice ran the numbers and gave me a spreadsheet showing the cash flow and debt for every company in the S&P 500.[25] Alice's list shows, for each company, the interest rates on their current debt that will turn them into a member of the walking dead.

Of course, debt will vary for each, but you can begin to imagine the carnage as sovereign debts and rising corporate debt spreads start exacting their toll.

> If you can't afford rent that's your fault for living in a city. Maybe if you lived in an open field or perhaps some kind of bog.
>
> — @InternetHippo

I don't wish to spend much time or effort on real estate, but somehow we managed to blow another bubble. It does not seem as frothy as the last—the 125 percent NINJA loans and condo-flipping TV shows seem subdued—but that may be because the purchases are being made by permanent capital (investors).

Whether current valuations and location of the debt pose a systemic risk is a question beyond my pay scale, but I am not sure you want to be exposed, since the largest landlords are pulling back on purchases to "ease away from the shifting housing market." [26] You want to be out of the splash zone when the likes of Blackrock start liquidating their positions because previous razor-thin profits boosted by huge leverage are no longer supported by near-zero interest rates. The world will be a better place when these predators are pushed back into their lairs.[27]

THE WALL STREET JOURNAL.

The homeowner association in the Whitehall Village neighborhood in Walkertown, N.C, wants to require new buyers to live in a home or leave it vacant for six months before renting it out.

Homeowner Groups Seek to Stop Investors From Buying Houses to Rent

After the total value of all cryptocurrencies reached an apex of just under $3 trillion last November – of which Bitcoin accounted for roughly $1.3 trillion – a rolling crash of epic proportions has wiped out more than two-thirds of that digital wealth. For crypto, however, there is no central bank standing by willing to bail out those who are caught up in the contagion.

— Doomberg

Cryptocurrencies. I would be remiss if I did not pay at least lip service to Bitcoin and the other cryptocurrencies, for it is a multi-trillion-dollar asset class that could cause unimaginable pleasure or pain.

Despite gargantuan efforts from the hodlers, I have not been converted. I may be, some day, but it will take a Battle of Bastards between the hodlers and the State, with the former staggering off the battlefield dazed but alive.

Microstrategy, a former tech stock turned bitcoin hedge fund, got brutalized as Bitcoin stock dove from $60,000 to $15,000. Surprisingly, Berkshire Hathaway lost billions by lending to Three Arrows Capital, a crypto hedge fund that collapsed. The Orifice of Omaha once again shows he does not just buy great companies. He is a stock jobber and, on a bad day, an asset tosher.

> I have said all along the crypto assets are highly speculative, very risky assets. My very humble assessment is that it is worth nothing. It is based on nothing, there is no underlying assets to act as an anchor of safety.
>
> — Christine Lagarde, spokesperson for the State, offering her very humble assessment

Bitcoin's problem may have been triggered by a number of calamities in the crypto underworld, where "shitcoins" reside unsupervised. The $60 billion network that markets LUNA tokens collapsed, sending $60 billion of perceived wealth back from whence it came.[28]

Stablecoins are like poker chips at the casino, except you cannot turn them in for dollars if murky grifters decided to squander the dollars while you speculated. The Terra stablecoin collapsed in minutes once its LUNA reserves collapsed.[29]

Ms. Lagarde called for a crackdown—first shot of the Battle of the Bastards?—because they are "based on nothing", and she understands the world of unbacked currencies.[30] Maybe she is too old; crypto seems to be a generational thing.

Terra's collapse brought attention to other larger and presumably more stable stablecoins. Although the Tether stablecoin is priced at parity—one Tether equals one dollar—it is said to be fractionally reserved (technically insolvent),[31] leading many to believe it will follow Terra down the blockdrain. Matt Taibbi ran an exposé on Circle Internet Financial, creators of the second-largest stablecoin, USDC, for running a Ponzi scheme.[32]

What would happen to the crypto market if the stablecoins went bits up is unclear even to the devout hodlers. They seem confident, but as in so many markets, confidence is everything and capricious.

> Crypto is basically a ponzi scheme, it's a way for really really really smart people to make money off of really smart people.
>
> — @MacroTalkGuy

The crypto index had a particularly bad day on June 13, 2022, dropping 22 percent. But don't count the bitcoin hodlers out. Lacking central banks to bail them out, they have already had more than their fair share of bungee jumps. Bitcoin's privacy got Ted Cruz's endorsement (FWIW),[33] while Edward Snowden suggests that there is nothing private about cryptos.[34] Reports of the FBI retrieving stolen bitcoins suggest that Ed is correct. Mark Jeftovic, a particularly astute hodler, notes that crypto assets held in accounts are subject to bankruptcy settlements.[35]

I watch with interest from the cheap seats.

> Luna fell 99% from $100 to $1. Then it fell another 99% from $1 to 1 cent. An important lesson here: if an asset falls 99%, it can still fall another 99%.
>
> — @fintwit_news

And that is all she wrote. *What?* Nothing about the collapse of FTX? Cool your jets. That is a story of corrupt geopolitics, not crypto.

ENERGY

> From deep within my conspiratorial mind emerged a theory about these contemporaneous supply constraints. No. Let's call it a narrative. If I was an Overlord and needed to sell a reluctant world on nuclear power, rather than patiently waiting for the plebes to get the memo, I would engineer a fossil fuel crisis—a cataclysmic one—to usher in the New Nuclear Age. I can imagine everybody squealing, "We need nuclear power to save us!" It worked for the vaccines. Mark my words—it's coming.[1]
>
> — me, in my Year in Review 2021

ALL THINGS CONSIDERED, that comment is now looking like a prophetic nugget of wisdom. Yet again, however, we face another topic from the Year in Transition in which our forward visibility is like peering through mashed potatoes. We will return to energy considerations in the sections on the war in Ukraine, but I have scrounged up other nuggets worth a ponder.

For starters, I see no evidence that fossil fuel production will ramp up to fill any voids. The regulators make us a capricious consumer. Political moods that change overnight, and a political tide that is decidedly going out and not coming in, have psychologically damaged an industry that must look at least ten years ahead in order to invest in big projects.

Meanwhile, our proxy war with *the* swing supplier (Russia), which is cozying up to the other swing supplier (Saudi Arabia),

---

is ominous. Even without the geopolitics, the enthusiasm of Aramco's CEO seems muted.

> Many of us have been insisting for years that if investments in oil and gas continued to fall, global supply growth would lag behind demand, impacting markets, the global economy, and people's lives. The increases this year are too little, too late, and too short-term. These are the real causes of this state of energy insecurity: under-investment in oil and gas; alternatives not ready; and no backup plan. But you would not know that from the response so far ... when the global economy recovers, we can expect demand to rebound further, eliminating the little spare oil production capacity out there. And by the time the world wakes up to these blind spots, it may be too late to change course. And at least this crisis has finally convinced people that we need a more credible energy transition plan.[2]
>
> — CEO of Aramco

Politics. Biden tapped the Strategic Petroleum Reserve (SPR) intended for national security to juice the midterm elections for the Democrats. It seems irresponsible.[3] Whether these are sales of real oil or only speculative tweaking of the futures market has been questioned.[4] He also threatened Big Oil with a special tax on their profits, which, I hasten to add, are non-existent when the price of oil drops and the producers continue to meet demand anyway.[5] Take away the profit incentive: Way to go, Brandon. At least you stemmed the red tide.

Democrats unveil plan to issue quarterly checks to Americans by taxing oil companies posting huge profits

Joseph Zeballos-Roig 15 hours ago

> Cornelius Vanderbilt made a profit of 14 cents from every barrel of flour shipped over his railroads. His efficiency lowered the price of flour for consumers. Did Vanderbilt keep any of you down by saving you $2.75 on a barrel of flour, while he was making 14 cents?[6]
>
> — Edward Atkinson, cotton magnate, 1886, to a group of workers

At the state level, California governor Gavin Newsom keeps making friends and influencing people on his Road to the White House by implementing bad ideas that are popular among the valley girls and boys. In his ascent of Mount Stupid, Gruesome Newsom banned water heaters and furnaces powered by natural gas in residential dwellings from 2030.[7]

He also went after Valero for "price gouging", that ever-popular war cry that is anathema to free markets and price discovery. Valero's counter-attack did not beat around the bush.[8] Gavin—may I call you Gavin?—wanted to impose a punitive tax on gasoline that he hoped would not be noticed by consumers at the pump.[9]

The effects of California's policies are self-evident.

Peak stupidity was attained when Gavin decided he would phase out gas-powered vehicles altogether. The same week, California power providers urged consumers not to overburden the grid when charging their cars.

Shale producers have been unable to secure financing in the new ESG grift. The Biden administration, after marinating in schadenfreude, found shortages and price hikes appalling now that there is a war, and demanded they open some spigot ... somewhere ... just do it.[10]

> Much of the social history of the Western world, over the past three decades, has been a history of replacing what worked with what sounded good.
>
> — Thomas Sowell

Electric vehicles. As the car manufacturers of the world chase Tesla into the future of gas-free vehicles, one can't help but wonder whether the grid will be ready, the bugs worked out, and the supplies for battery production located. I am told EVs are a hoot to drive. Toyota seems to stand alone in suggesting that the world is not ready yet.[11,12]

- Here is a nice analysis of the cost and energy demands of electric cars—a bean count of the hydrocarbons required to make the cars and batteries.[13] The Hofferian green fanatics tend to overlook the energy costs of hauling 500,000 pounds of ore from mile-deep open-pit mines in a faraway land to make one EV, while marveling at the absence of a tailpipe.
- The 2023 Chevy Bolt EV retails at $26,595. After an estimated 70,000 miles, the replacement battery is

projected to cost $29,842 based on *today's price*.[14] At least you can charge it on your Visa card.

- Imagine the chaos of a million electric cars running out of power while their occupants flee a hurricane zone. Once you clean up the carcasses, there remain cars to charge or tow rather than just pouring a can of gas in the tank. (Actually, my mechanic told me submersion of a car—a computer with wheels—after my wife drove one into a swamp.) Senators are pushing a bill to electrify the military vehicle fleet and retrofit all submarines with screen doors.[15]

> We should focus on the issue of electric school buses. I was proud to introduce the first piece of legislation to electrify our nation's fleet of school buses.
>
> — Kamala Harris

Shortages. On the international scene, Europe looks like it could be heating homes by burning tires this winter as the war in Ukraine puts energy out of most people's price range, and possibly unattainable at any price. After Germany dumped its politically incorrect nuclear plants, it discovered that alternative energies aren't worth shit. With Russian gas supplies cut off thanks to the U.S. blowing up the Nord Stream 2 pipeline, Europe is facing a harsh winter.[16] Deforesting the countryside for firewood is a step back to the Neolithic era.[17] Of course, the German greens illustrate the power of the new strains of weed by supporting coal over nuclear energy.[18]

Well, at least Germany can ship energy up the Rhine River. Scratch that; the water levels are too low this year.[19] The energy-savvy Doomberg (the pseudonym for a guy with serious credentials in his former career) says even if Germans fill their storage capacity to the brim it won't cover their needs. The Saker agrees.[20] Energy-consuming smokestack industries are planning for shutdowns.[21]

In 2018, then-President Trump warned Germany not to depend on Russia, while the German delegation overtly snickered.[22] When the winter is over, we will find out who gets the last laugh. As George W. Bush might say, "The Germans have no word for 'schadenfreude.'"[23]

German Chancellor Gerhard Schröder pushed Germany away from clean and efficient nuclear power and into the dependence of Russia's gas. It's hard to believe he is now Chairman of Russia's Rosneft and was added to Gazprom's board 20 days before Putin's invasion.

— Kyle Bass (@jkylebass), CIO of Hayman Capital

The rest of the Europeans are not happy cloggers either. Belgian think tank fellow Simone Tagliapietra astutely noted, "We have no interest in energy prices causing instability in member states—it would be a recipe for disaster."[24] Since Europe has a long and glorious history of peace and tranquility, this is no big deal, right? Let me fire a few bullets of my own.

- France is about to nationalize the last 14 percent of its major state-owned energy company as half of its reactors are being taken offline. France has flipped from being an energy exporter to an importer into a tight market.[25]
- BP owned a 20 percent stake in Rosneft before the West cut off its nose to spite its face and disowned Russian energy companies. Although its profits will hold up, owing to higher prices, production will not.[26]
- Diesel shortages in the U.S. are jacking up the cost of shipping all those goods delivered by Amazon.com as well as diverting diesel exports to Europe.[27] There are rumors that the shortage could last at least a year. Why?
- Other U.S. energy supplies are looking unreliable as well.[28] Maybe we can squeegee out the bottom of the SPR in a pinch.

> Many think we will subsidize our way to renewables, but we won't, for inherently physical reasons. Sunlight & wind are too energy-dilute. Solar/wind projects need ~300x more land, 300% more copper, and 700% more rare earths than fossil fuels, making them prohibitively expensive.[29]
>
> — Michael Shellenberger, prominent environmentalist

Renewable energies. Before you get all teary-eyed about replacing fossil fuels with alternatives low in energy density, let's look at the renewables. I remind you that if we take fossil fuels offline and fail to fill the void, we will suffer a catastrophic drop in the quality and quantity of life. Bill Gates and his vaccine-happy eugenics buddies spewing scary chestnuts about culling the herd might be passing out invites to the Donner Holiday Party. Albert Bartlett's lectures on our failure to understand exponential functions beautifully illustrate the limits to growth.[30]

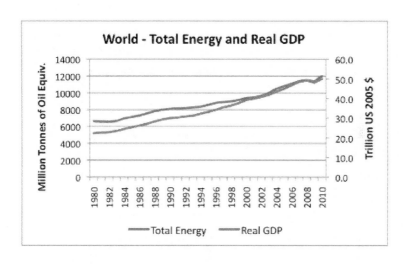

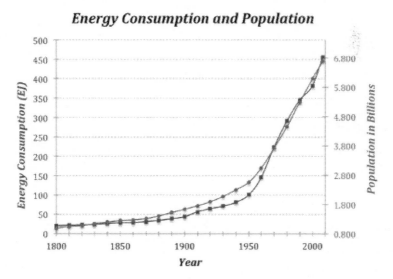

I'll repeat what I have written repeatedly about climate change, starting in 2019.[31] I do not believe the climate narrative and am highly doubtful that we can pull off the transition to clean energy without nukes.

Let's just bullet a few more observations—throw a few more logs on the fire.

- Solar power enthusiasts should note that solar panels function optimally at around 25°C and become less efficient as they heat up. Maybe this idea of covering Arizona with panels is linear thinking in a non-linear world.[32]
- Here is a link to a nice tutorial on why alternative energies have barely moved the needle and how the environmentally destructive mining industry will have to ramp up one thousand percent.[33] This analysis claims they can't even work theoretically.[34]
- Australia is the largest coal producer in the world but has gone green by legislating coal-powered electricity out of existence. Without a reliable energy supply, their grid and energy markets are unstable.[35]
- Art Berman, whose analyses garner widespread respect, says that oil has a thousand-fold advantage over solar when one considers the labor force required to produce the same amount of energy.[36] Think of solar as a government jobs program.

Perhaps this entire section is drivel from a peak oiler suffering from confirmation bias, but to accept the alternative narratives without careful analysis is reckless.

> There is not the slightest indication that [nuclear energy] will ever be obtainable. It would mean that the atom would have to be shattered at will.
>
> — Albert Einstein, 1932

Nukes. I've concluded that we've all got to grow a pair and embrace nuclear power. The climate changers who support nuclear to solve the perceived CO_2 problem are at least consistent. Those who wish to reduce CO_2 without nukes are Hofferian fanatics lacking a clue.

Whether you are a neophyte or a semi-literate energy buff, I recommend Justin Huhn's (@uraniuminsider) two-part tutorial on Wealthion, covering all facets of nuclear energy.[37] He covers the brilliance of second-generation nukes (SMRs), the red herring of waste disposal, sourcing uranium (including from discarded mine tailings), the distant (currently unreachable) promise of thorium and fusion, and investment opportunities.

Recall that I entered the uranium investment world in late 2020—a dollar and a dream. The case for nuclear is quite strong.

- Coal plants release a hundred times more uranium and thorium into the environment than do the world's 440 nuclear reactors.[38]
- Japan experienced the Hiroshima and Nagasaki bombings, and the Fukushima disaster in 2011, yet they are embracing nuclear power once again.[39]
- China is supplying the world with solar panels and windmills to pay for the two dozen nuclear power plants under construction and the hundred more in the planning

stages.[40] Why don't they just keep the solar panels and windmills?

- UK Prime Minister Boris "BoJo" Johnson "went nuclear" before leaving office, promising $810 million seed money for the Sizewell C nuclear power project. "It always looks relatively expensive to build and to run, but look at what's happening today, look at the results of Putin's war ... I say go nuclear, and go large." The head-scratcher is that the $24 billion project will be funded by a French- and Chinese-owned energy company.[41]

Disclose.tv
@disclosetv

NEW - Greta Thunberg calls the possible shutdown of nuclear power plants in Germany a mistake.

THE COLLAPSE OF FTX

> I've had a bad month.
>
> — Sam Bankman-Fried

THE FTX CRYPTO EXCHANGE COLLAPSE is not a crypto story. There are overviews that probe the darkness,[1,2,3] but I suspect the unassailable truth will prove elusive because the roots of this story burrow deeply into geopolitics.

FTX, briefly the world's second-largest crypto exchange, was domiciled in the Bahamas. The largest exchange (Binance) is domiciled in China, so your spidey sense should already be tingling. Referred to as the "Gang of Kids," the FTX team and its partner in crime, hedge fund Alameda Research, seem to have come from nowhere—zero to sixty faster than a Tesla.

Well, in 2022 they went back from sixty to zero, like a Tesla hitting a bridge abutment. In doing so they depleted the wealth of some serious investors, including the likes of Tom Brady, Sequoia Capital, and Softbank's Masayoshi Son, the Mr. Miyagi of scandals and wealth destruction.[4] (FTX is a $100 million drop in the bucket of Masayoshi's $5 billion personal deficit.)

At the center is a whizz-kid named Sam Bankman-Fried, now known as Sam Bankman-Fraud (SBF), a boy genius from MIT—aren't they all?—touted as the second coming of Jesus Christ (Warren Buffett). Heads up, SBF: you are sitting too close to Bill Clinton.

SBF participated in a *New York Times*-sponsored panel discussion *after the collapse.*[5] That lineup of participants certainly gets my neurons firing.

The New York Times **Events**

November 30, 2022, 8 a.m.–6 p.m. E.S.T.
New York City
Premier Sponsor Accenture

Speakers

Sam Bankman-Fried
C.E.O., FTX

President Volodymyr Zelensky
Ukraine

Larry Fink
Chairman and C.E.O., BlackRock

Secretary Janet L. Yellen
U.S. Department of the Treasury

Mysterious successes. Nobody seems to know who bankrolled SBF. The FTX in-house cryptocurrency, FTT, was pumped to lofty levels, which is trivial to do even without real buyers, but it was then monetized into real dollar-denominated wealth. Serious money and well-orchestrated moral support began rolling in.

It has all the trappings of a campaign run by an elite public relations firm, painting Sam as both a monetary genius and uber-altruist.[6] The gang at FTX were quite the philanthropists, giving money to non-profits to save the world from the evils of climate change [7] and global pandemics,[8] and to the anti-Trump

Lincoln Project[9] and rising authoritarians in Russia.[10] Sam produced galaxy-class performative virtue signaling.[11] His cultish worldview is called "effective altruism" although "altruistic sociopathy" seems more appropriate.

A letter signed by San Francisco Fed President Mary Daly, inducting the Farmington State Bank, recently purchased by SBF's team, into the Federal Reserve System—the Big Leagues—shows their gravitas.[12]

The players. Before getting into the weeds about what these Jolt Cola-swilling codeheads were *really* doing, let's just gander at some of the key players.

Sam Bankman-Fried (SBF): Despite his image as an MIT-graduated genius and all-around good guy, SBF is said to be a "spoiled, sadistic, hedonistic, and ruthlessly dishonest bully of a manchild"[13] with a penchant for drug-fueled orgies.[14] He should have gone into politics.

Caroline Ellison: CEO of FTX sister company (and hedge fund) Alameda Research, and ex-girlfriend of SBF. She looks like a recent middle-school graduate (and might wish to try some shampoo). She is said to be a once-geeky, brilliant high school student who must have crossed over to the dark side while at Stanford, eventually meeting SBF at a trading firm, Jane Street. The one interview I watched made her look like a total nitwit.[15]

Joseph Bankman: Father of Sam (not to be confused with Son of Sam). A Stanford professor with tax law experience who has lobbied Congress on behalf of hedge funds.[16] He brings game to the group. He was present when Sam was picked up by the police in the Bahamas.

Gabe Bankman-Fried: This illustrious gene pool includes Sam's brother Gabe, who, as a former Jane Street trader, founded Guardian Against Pandemics, a seemingly underfunded super PAC supporting leftist organizations to facilitate pandemic response.[17,18] The geopolitical implications of COVID suggest that a deeper dive may prove fruitful. The plot thickener is that he has lobbied Congress and has links to DNC donors. He worked for Democrat Congressman Sean Casten of Illinois, who is on the committee that oversees cryptocurrencies and initial coin offerings (ICOs).[19]

Barbara Bankman-Fried: Sam's mom is not only Hillary Clinton's lawyer but also co-founder of Mind the Gap, a fundraising organization that pushed $20 million to the DNC for the 2020 election and helped promote mail-in voting.[20]

Linda Fried: Otherwise known as Aunt Linda. She is on the Global Agenda Council on Aging and is a member of Klaus Schwab's WEF,[21] which may have cemented FTX's ties with the WEF.

Glenn Ellison: Father of Caroline. Obviously brilliant in his role as a professor of economics at the top-ranked MIT econ department.[22] Critically, he also worked for Gary Gensler (*vide infra*).

FTX

FTX is a cryptocurrency exchange built by traders, for traders. FTX offers innovative products including industry-first derivatives, options, volatility products and leveraged tokens. It strives to develop a platform robust enough for professional trading firms and intuitive enough for first-time users.

Gary Gensler: As the Head of the Securities and Exchange Commission (SEC), Gary has critical connections that would have been useful to SBF, the son of his former employee, Joseph Bankman. Like SBF's mother, Gensler has ties to the Clinton Foundation and as Hillary's political advisor.[23]

Sam Trabucco: He has a reputation for being a great gambler and game player, getting started professionally at the Susquehanna International Group (SIG), the world's largest equity options trading firm. As a big picture guy, Sam must have understood the troubles at FTX and Alameda.

Amy Wu: Amy is a cross-town Harvard grad. As the FTX Head of Ventures & Commercial at FTX Ventures, Amy is yet another Clinton Foundation trainee.[24]

Mark Wetjen: FTX's head of Policy and Regulation was Obama's Commissioner of Commodity Futures Trading and acting chair of the CFTC following Gensler's departure.[25]

You should be sensing a pattern. FTX is a geopolitically connected organization that moves (launders) money. Some of its actions were simple graft and corruption. SBF's parents bought $121 million in Bahamian real estate over the past two years with funds provided by FTX.[26] SBF's affiliated Alameda Research appears to have been front-running crypto announcements before listing them on FTX.[27] Nothing crooked here. Some believe they were behind the crypto collapses mentioned in Broken Markets (above). Alameda extended loans to SBF ($1 billion), and to two affiliates who received $543 million and $55 million.[28]

> While this partnership was touted as a way to assist Ukraine in cashing out crypto donations for ammunition and humanitarian aid, we have serious concerns that the Ukrainian government may have invested portions of the nearly $66 billion of U.S. economic assistance into FTX to keep Democrats in power—and keep the money coming in.[29]
>
> — Republican lawmakers, writing to Antony Blinken

The DNC landed an estimated $69 million of *visible* donations from FTX leadership, according to Forbes.[30] There is no way to know if the quoted numbers are accurate or a tip of the iceberg. A video of Maxine Waters blowing SBF a kiss would be embarrassing, if any of these sociopaths were capable of embarrassment.[31]

The RNC is not completely off the hook. Several Republicans received gifts, including Mitch McConnell.[32] You may have heard that Mitch gave no financial support to Kari Lake in the Arizona elections. Meanwhile, FTX was supporting

Kari Lake's opponent, Katie Hobbs, who "won" in a highly contested election that was under the strict supervision of ... Katie Hobbs.[33] One suspects that FTX's financial problems were buried until after the elections.

> Crypto assets proved extremely helpful in facilitation of funding flows to Ukrainian citizens and soldiers, as well as in raising awareness and engaging people worldwide.[34]
>
> — Oleksandr Bornyakov, an official at the Ukraine digital ministry

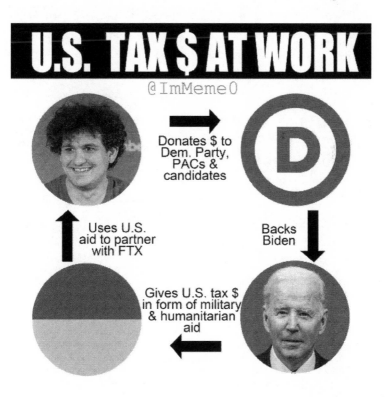

Ukraine and FTX partnered on a crypto-based website to enable donations to be made to Ukraine's war effort, with the proceeds going to the National Bank of Ukraine.[35] U.S. "military aid" also made it to the Clintonskyy Fund—OK, I made that up—and was invested in FTT cryptocoin by Kiev.[36,37]

A Ukraine-based money laundering scheme is discussed, away from polite company.[38] Here is how it works: Biden sends money to Ukraine, Ukraine uses FTX to send money back to the DNC, and the DNC ensures "10 percent for the Big Guy."

In a surreal twist, a hodler-based Twitter Space, running 24/7 tracking breaking news about SBF and FTX, took a break to have a guest speaker—Hunter Biden.[39] A friend and punk, Wall Street Silver (@WallStreetSilv), brought up the subject of the laptop and was immediately banished.[40] Makes you wonder where the veiled purchasers of Hunter's over-priced art were domiciled. All roads lead to Ukraine.

COVID is both a medical and geopolitical narrative. FTX funded research into "repurpose therapy"—finding old drugs that solve new problems—for the pandemic. Yet somehow they never supported hydroxychloroquine or Ivermectin.[41] FTX sponsored the Together Trial, which was bought-and-paid-for crap designed to discredit Ivermectin.[42] The fact-checkers call this hooey, which means it's probably true. "Guarding Against Pandemics", a group that lobbies for government money to prevent pandemics, was founded by Gabe Bankman-Fried. It's yet another grift. SBF and his team wanted a mere $30 billion out of the Biden administration.[43]

The collapse. So was the collapse of FTX to become BRE-FTX (sorry: a gold joke), like every other Ponzi scheme, due to its inability to bring in more cash? I see little evidence that cash flow was a problem. I think many must have known it was a scam, but my buddy Marc Cohodes, known for his slash-and-burn short-selling skills, is getting credit for calling bullshit during a Hedgeye podcast in which he tore FTX a new one in his unique style.[44] Binance tried to save FTX but then backed out, and that was the fatal headshot. When The Wolfman (John Ray III) was called in to clean up the post-collapse wreckage, he found no risk control, not even a real corporate structure.[45] He had helped clean up Enron, and said FTX was even worse. There are thousands of crypto buffs out there, and they are now a pack of cadaver dogs looking for the corpses.

> Never in my career have I seen such a complete failure of corporate controls and such a complete absence of trustworthy financial information as occurred here.
>
> —John Ray III

It was obvious within a day or two that this was not a financial scandal, prompting the following tweet.

Dave "All Roads Lead to Ukraine" Collum
@DavidBCollum

Before this FTX scandal is over, I predict that there will be bodies washing up on beaches around the world. This is not a financial story.

11:47 AM · Nov 16, 2022

That was a good guess, but unbeknownst to me it had already started. A small handful of players in the crypto world took unplanned trips into the Great Blockchain Beyond.[46,47,48,49,50] (I don't know the total.) One was frantically declaring he was about to be framed.[51] He should have been so lucky. Recall those orgies within the FTX team? I'm getting that faint pizza smell. One hodler was sounding the alarm about pedophile rings, the CIA, and the Mossad—very Epsteinish.[52] He *literally* washed up on a beach.

This plotline goes very deep and dark. It is not suitable for children or the faint of heart[53] and it is unclear if it will contribute to the Clinton Body Count.

Maxine Wat... ✔ & **U.S. House Committee on Financial Servi...** ✔ ···
@RepMaxineWaters & @FSCDems

.@SBF_FTX, we appreciate that you've been candid in your discussions about what happened at #FTX. Your willingness to talk to the public will help the company's customers, investors, and others. To that end, we would welcome your participation in our hearing on the 13th.

10:01 AM · Dec 2, 2022

CNN ✔
@CNN

breaking news

4:28 PM · Sep 1, 2022 · Twitter Web App

608 Retweets   **504** Quote Tweets   **2,369** Likes

> The FTX founder pledged to donate billions. His firm's swift collapse wiped out his wealth and ambitious philanthropic endeavors.
>
> — The *Wall Street Journal*, intentionally missing the point

The media. Displaying the authenticity of a stepmom on Pornhub, the media showed how deep the rot is by soft-pedaling the story.[54] The headlines read like a *Leave It to Beaver* episode in which The Beave yet again gets himself into a bind. What have those silly gooses gotten into now? Sam said he doesn't remember comingling the funds, and sounds implausibly clueless for a boy genius. He was selling the sweet, innocent schtick pretty hard.

It seems odd that a Madoff-scale scammer is walking the streets. On the other hand, Zerohedge pointed out that there are 6,300 documented corporate frauds that led to fines and no jail time.[55] Only suckers go to jail. It is *bizarre* that he was still tweeting, doing interviews with Andrew Ross Sorkin and Clinton crony George Stephanopoulos,[56,57,58] and fielding ridiculous questions with ridiculous answers on Twitter Spaces.[59] Was this faux openness under the advice of legal counsel, or is he simply *that* confident that he cannot be touched?

Let me tell you something, Sam: you could be written out of this plot *very* quickly. Timmy's life expectancy would have been squat, had Lassie not been there to save his ass. Who is saving yours? In the end, inconvenient people will be silenced, and this story will just go away like all the others. Fuck 'em.

> Internet trolls are scapegoating Sam, but we should celebrate entrepreneurs even when they fail. There's nothing illegal about taking big risks.[60]
>
> — Andrew Ross Sorkin, streetwalker, defending this generation's Bernie Madoff

Conclusion. So where does this take us? Some suspect it is a hitjob on Bitcoin to usher in central bank digital currencies (CBDCs). The authorities began discussions of regulation almost immediately. It smacks of global money laundering looks like the story. We also have absolutely no idea of the depth and breadth of this malignant tumor. We can see only the surface, not the roots. The headline losses in the tens of billions of dollars may not reflect the total flows passing through FTX and Ukraine.

CAL	GEOR	ALASKA
HAW	SC	WASH
ARIZ	NC	IDAHO
NEV	VIRG	MONTAN
UTAH	WVA	WYOM
COLO	MARY	N. DAK
TEX	PENNS	S. DAK
KANS	NY	MINN
MO	NJ	ARKANS
WISC	MAINE	IOWA
MICH	MASS	NEBRAS
OHIO	OREG	N. HAMP
ILLI	DELAWAR	OKLAHOM
IND		DELAWR
KENT		CONN
TENN	D.C.	N. MEX
ALAB		R.I.
LOUIS		
MISSIS		
FLOR		

CLIENT PROFILE INSTRUCTIONS

ew Client or Existing Client:
ofile or this is a different registration type or financial

eviously provided on the Client Profile.

ity account.

CUSTODIAL

IRA-Educational
IRA-Minor Fiduciary
Guardianship/Conservatorship
UGMA UTMA
UGMA 529

nts for each.)

Trust Under Agreement
Trust Under Will
Unincorporated Entity
**Retirement Plans

SA and Non-ERISA Retirement Plans.

ult with your financial professional if you are unsure

Lest we forget, some of those were savings of Joe and Jane Sixpack *stolen and given to the friends of the DNC and global elite.* Retail hodlers knowingly took on risk, but not *that* risk. The Biden administration was asked about giving the millions back to help investors recoup their losses, and his press agent ducked the question. The DNC keeps plumbing new lows. Just as the boy genius was scheduled to testify to Congress, to the consternation of the DNC, he got scooped up by Bahamian authorities and put in their DNC-sponsored witness protection program. Sam Bankman-Epstein (SBE) is now in good hands.

NEWS NUGGETS

I RUN ACROSS news stories that capture my imagination, make me cringe, or elicit a chuckle. (I will *never* say "LOL.") Usually they are categorized, but this year I am just mashing them together into a Hungarian goulash of human folly. Others worthy of more detailed analysis show up in later sections. Some are not for the faint of heart, so if you have a personality disorder or are a member of the fanatical wing of the Democratic party, you might want to read somebody else's book; maybe one pushing climate change.

- Kyle Rittenhouse is suing the hell out of everybody who smeared him for his self-defense in the Kenosha, WI riots.[1]
- A high school kid got to sub for Pearl Jam's drummer when the drummer got sick.[2]
- Nancy Pelosi's husband, Paul, seems to have a lively social life with some lingering personal issues. Soon after a DUI, with some suspicious details being left largely undiscussed, he managed to get himself into a tryst with a dude named David. The scramble to change the narrative ignored a window broken from the inside, a police audio saying that they seemed to know each other, and BLM posters hung in the abode of this putative QAnon assailant.[3] A prominent NBC reporter suggested the story was complex and got suspended.[4] Let's posit that Paul's a perv with a drinking problem: who cares? Protecting Paul's image is one thing, but trying to flip it to a midterm election talking point about white supremacy is pathological. As Joseph Welch said to Joe McCarthy, "Have you no sense of decency?"

So if we're to believe the media...

A rainbow flag waving nudist prostitute got up at 2am Friday morning

Decided to create 2 random websites with hundreds of posts about Q Anon and big brother in the dead of night

Then stripped down to his underwear, grabbed a hammer, and JOGGED all the way to Nancy Pelosi's house

And, miraculously, breached two layers of max level Secret Service security designed to protect the third most powerful person in the world, with nothing but a hammer and some tightly whities

And finally shouted "WHERE'S NANCY!!" before smacking Paul in the head with a hammer, in front of cops, without being absolutely riddled bullets

This guy is basically fucking Jason Bourne apparently

He could breach two layers of federal security in an assassination attempt but didn't bother to check if Nancy was even in the country 😄 😄 lol ok

- Ghislaine "Jizz" Maxwell got 20 years for sex trafficking under-aged girls ... to nobody. Makes you wonder why the rampant trafficking of children over the Southern border never leads to the conviction of *any* pervs. These kids can't be cheap. Balenciaga! Speaking of pervs, it appears as though we got the flight logs to the Lolita Express, although confirming this is tough. Its veracity is questionable because Bill Clinton is only on there 28 times.[5] Prince Andrew settled out of court with the former 17-year-old Virginia Giuffre.[6] The Epstein–Maxwell story has largely been shoved back down the memory hole, enabling racketeers and politically powerful pedophiles to soil the world in perpetuity.

- We named one of our new warships the USS Fallujah.[7]
- As we mourned the loss of the Queen of England it is easy to overlook the challenges the new king faces, living without mum.

 **Wall Street Silver** ✓
@WallStreetSilv

First day without his mom, look at the buttons on his suit jacket

7:12 PM · Sep 17, 2022 · Twitter Web App

2,535 Retweets   **232** Quote Tweets   **22.3K** Likes

- Anne Heche died in a flaming car crash. She was said to be working on a documentary about Jeffrey Epstein, but of course the fact-checkers disagree.[8] Neither Michael Hastings [9,10] nor Seth Rich [11] were available for comment.

- A former Clinton advisor and link to Epstein hanged himself from a tree and then shot himself in the chest twice with a shotgun (or vice versa). There was no investigation.[12] The Clinton Body Count—deaths proximate to the Clinton Machine that do not involve bombing the shit outta some foreign land and which have been fact-checked more than any story in history—exceeds 160.[13] Jimmy Carter didn't get close to that number, even if you include the entire U.S. military under his command.

- Gender activists are pressuring anthropologists to stop referring to human remains as "male" or "female".[14] People with Neanderthal roots—the red-heads [15] pejoratively referred to as "carrot tops"—have been calling for reparations.

> For the record I made women from men before it was cool.
>
> — God @TheTweetOfGod

- California wingnuts became agitated when "militia groups" showed up to help people evacuate during the forest fires.[16] Sounds like the Cajun Navy.[17]

- Alex Jones lost $50 million in a court case for pushing hard (too far?) on the Sandy Hook story,[18] but not before calling out the Clintons and Alex Epstein in court, creating quite a meme.[19] He then lost again, with damages approaching a billion dollars. I might be able to see past the First

Amendment issues to find damages, but a billion bucks? I bet a court will undo most of that. The free speech issues will linger. Robbie Parker was not available for comment.

Reuters Legal ✓
@ReutersLegal

Jury says Alex Jones must pay $965 million in second Sandy Hook defamation trial

- George Jetson was born on July 31, 2022.[20]
- CNN launched a pay-to-play streaming service called CNN+. The 10,000 subscribers was a tad short of their projected 29 million,[21] causing an NFL-quality punt following the $300 million fumble.[22] Rumor must have leaked that Brian "the Potato" Stelter, Chris Cuomo, and John Harwood would be leaving without "letting the door hit them in their asses."[23] Technically, Cuomo is not gone but was demoted to the mailroom. A 2018 clip surfaced of Ted Koppel explaining to the Potato that he basically sucks and would be nothing without Trump.[24]
- Two years ago I set out to understand China's role in global politics. China is completely opaque. I've got nothing. This troubles me, like when the kids are upstairs and they are being quiet.
- Giorgia Meloni, far-right firebrand, was elected prime minister of Italy. The European power structure painted her as a fascist, but even her opponent, Matteo Renzi, said, "She is my rival, and we will continue to fight each other, but the idea that now there is a risk of fascism in Italy is absolutely fake news."[25] The curdling of European leaders' blood can only be understood by listening to her tear into

Macron[26,27] and the European power structure[28,29] with savagery rarely seen outside divorce courts.[30,31] Get ready for subtitles, but turn up the volume on her speeches. Then listen to this imitation of her and try not to laugh.[32]

> We will see the result of the vote in Italy. If things go in a difficult direction—and I've spoken about Hungary and Poland—we have the tools.[33]
>
> — Ursula Von der Leyen, president of the EU

- Sam Brinton, the "gender fluid" Biden appointee responsible for disposal of nuclear waste and clearly a breakthrough appointment for the LGBTQ community, kept stealing jewelry from luggage at the airport.[34] Jackie Robinson played his historically profound role with greater grace and dignity.

- A fast-food restaurant customer pulled an axe out of his bag and did some physical damage to the establishment,[35] giving diners a story to tell their grandchildren and CNN something to talk about other than Paul Pelosi and fake laptops. If you search "brawls at [fill in the blank]" you will find this is routine. The media obsessed over his release soon thereafter, not noticing that the laws left the judge no choice.[36] As an aside, I watched the video and saw a guy getting repeatedly punched before doing his Bernie Goetz imitation.[37] I hope the court mandates a switch to decaf for the mischievous lad.

- The Onion filed a Supreme Court brief in support of a man who was arrested and prosecuted for making fun of police on social media. True to form, it is written satirically.[38,39]

- Elon Musk was on fire during his hostile raid on Twitter, threatening to buy Coke and put the cocaine back in,[40] calling out the absence of Epstein's contacts,[41] and chiding Hillary for possibly overlooking some nagging details in her defense of Paul "the Perve" Pelosi, sending the fact-checkers into overdrive.[42] The Left went batshit when he uttered the phrase "all lives matter." And then he bought Twitter. This story is playing out too fast to follow right now, but it is clear that the Twitter Stasi guided by the DNC were as oppressive as everybody already knew.[43] It is a year in transition.

> Elon could actually control what people think ... that is our job.
>
> — Mika Brzezinski, MSNBC

- The COO of the fake meat company, Beyond Meat, was arrested for biting a man's nose. Isn't a nose, technically speaking, meat?[44]
- Tennis star Novak Djokovic set a new high-water mark in sports by being banned for not doing drugs.[45] He says he will skip all events that require vaccination.[46]
- Loose cannon and Shankster Phil Mickelson made some unfiltered remarks about the new Saudi-backed golf tour offering huge paydays. "They're scary motherf— to get involved with. We know they killed Khashoggi and have a horrible record on human rights. They execute people over there for being gay."[47] Loose lips sink ships. After some further thought and maybe some guidance, he asked rhetorically, "Why would I even consider it? Because this is a once-in-a-lifetime opportunity to reshape how the PGA Tour operates."

- A horse named Rich Strike won the Kentucky Derby at odds of 80:1.
- A 29-year-old trans woman dominated a girl's skateboarding competition, whipping the asses of 10–16-year-olds. It is a beautiful story of inclusion, in which the evil forces of ageism were battled and defeated.[48]
- Congratulations to transgender swimmer Lia Thomas, who, after being beaten by Yale's transgender swimmer,[49] went on to win gold at the NCAA swimming championships. It is said that the silver medalists are the least happy of the three medalists. Truer words were never spoken, with pictures telling the story.

- University officials announced that Lia's teammates were not available for comment.[50] I would also like to give the women's athletic establishment a silver medal for all the words that were never spoken in defense of women's sports. Alas, y'all failed to meet the minimum requirement for participation trophies.

- Amy Coney Barrett's performance to get the Supreme Court nod in 2021 was near perfection until she signed a $425,000 book deal.[51] Other justices had written memoirs, but doing so before adjudicating her first case leaves a bad taste in my mouth. The left condemned it because they hate the Roe v. Wade call.[52]

- A chess champion has been accused of cheating. Since saying, "Hey! Look over there!" and moving a piece won't work, he cheated by receiving new-era Morse Code from an electronic device jammed up his ass.[53] The scandal caused quite a buzz. As to who was sending the signals is unclear, but my bet is on Big Blue.

- Climate activists—Hoffer's truest believers—began defacing some of history's great artwork or gluing themselves to paintings.[54,55] Buy a dozen tasers and charge museum goers twenty bucks a pop; you could buy a da Vinci with the proceeds. For the five who glued themselves to the floor in a Porsche dealership, just lock the doors and turn out the lights.[56] As to those blocking traffic at crowded intersections, I would think studded snow tires would send the right message.

- Santa Claus's tomb (Saint Nicholas's, actually) was found under a church in Turkey.[57]

- Will Smith smacked Chris Rock at the Academy Awards. Using Wall Street parlance, that called the top in his career. Minutes later he won the Academy Award, right before being hurled into the Crack of Doom by peers who are paid millions to simulate violence and sexual assault for entertainment. The whole thing looked staged to me (and others)—they were friends—but Rock never came to his defense. He should have, even if it was unstaged. That is what a friend would do.

- The average Academy Awards nominee spends $1.5 million on their outfit.[58] (I presume this price is for the women's gowns.) It is ironic, given the content of their acceptance speeches.

- My colleague John McMurry, author of the largest-selling organic chemistry textbook in the world, outfoxed the publishing world by releasing his tenth and final edition for free, in memory of his recently departed son.[59,60]

- With a throw from deep right field, Matt Walsh released a documentary entitled, "What is a Woman?"[61] He somehow managed to ignite a bench-clearing brawl that brought the transgender movement into view.[62] Opponents of the movement,[63] non-statistically populated with parents, started throwing punches at the gender benders for pushing too far too fast. Bill Maher jumped in,[64] suggesting it is radical to do surgery on a kid struggling with whether to be a cowboy or princess. So did the more credible but less humorous UK National Health Service.[65] A video surfaced of a woman at Vanderbilt University's Medical Center salivating at a podium about the enormous profit from what Walsh calls "castrations."[66] (More profitable than normal surgeries?) Soon, Vanderbilt and other medical centers with clinics that specialize in "gender-affirming hysterectomies" and related interventions on minors[67,68] were frantically doing radical website reconstructive surgeries, removing critical parts with hacksaws. (Coda: the guy who invented lobotomies won the Nobel Prize.[69]) And, like clockwork, Governor Gavin Newsom declared California a sanctuary state for minors interested in such surgeries without parental permission.[70] He wants to be your next president. If a doc did that to my kid without my permission, I would do some gender-adjusting surgery too.

- Maitland Jones, a former Princeton tenured professor and current NYU adjunct organic chemistry professor, was fired after students petitioned to have him removed because his class was "bitchin' hard", causing a high attrition rate.[71] It could be true—he was old guard in a field populated with demanding researchers—and high attrition certainly poses a problem. He was also 84 years old, so he may not have been at the top of his game. The unreported part of the story that I believe is irrelevant but still at least ironic, is that the president of NYU, Andy Hamilton (a friend), was denied tenure at Princeton while Maitland was on the faculty. I am confident the firing had nothing to do with Andy because the decision was surely made at low—sub-faculty—levels, and Andy does not have a vindictive bone in his body. But, as Paul Harvey would say, "And now you know the rest of the story."

- Governor DeSantis shipped several dozen immigrants to a self-described "sanctuary" at Martha's Vineyard. I thought it was funnier than hell, but the DNC political machine had a cow. Get over it: the Biden administration had been flying them around the country covertly for two years.[72] The Vineyardians declared that the sanctuary thing was a theoretical construct and had the immigrants' sorry asses sent back to the mainland 34 hours later.

- Mount Royal University in Canada canceled ice hockey intramurals owing to inadequate "equity, diversity, and inclusion." [73] What were those hosers thinking, eh?
- Ilya Shapiro, Executive Director and Senior Lecturer at Georgetown Law School, beat the university in a free-speech suit and then resigned, noting, "You've made it impossible for me to fulfill my duties of my appointed post." [74]
- The CEO of Kraken, a crypto tech company, offered a severance package to employees who felt "triggered by controversial ideas". [75] Kraken's updated mission statement suggests "the ideal Krakenite is thick-skinned and well-

intentioned." Krakenite sure sounds like space-age durability.

- PayPal decided it would be cool to deduct up to $2,500 from the accounts of those providing misinformation on key issues.[76] The uproar caused them to backpedal on the idea,[77] but that bell cannot be unrung. Marc Jeftovic does a fine deep-dive on the authoritarian underpinnings.[78] PayPal then reinstated the policy.[79]

Dave "All Roads Lead to Ukraine" Collum
@DavidBCollum   · · ·

That Paypal has backed away from their plan to doc your bank account up to $2,500 on social media for posting misinformation is a bell that cannot be un-rung. It is foreshadowing of authoritarianism. Possibly unstoppable. It was a good run to now.

12:07 PM · Oct 9, 2022

iIiI View Tweet analytics

486 Retweets   **32** Quote Tweets   **3,014** Likes

- Psychologists say that victimhood virtue signalers score high in the Dark Triad traits: Machiavellianism, Narcissism, and Psychopathy.[80,81]
- Netflix employee protests over Dave Chappelle's stand-up comedy show, "The Closer," led management to tell them to quit the censorship crap or take a hike. "If you'd find it hard to support our content breadth, Netflix may not be the best place for you." By the way, Netflix is hemorrhaging money now that lockdowns are over and expensive content creation is back in vogue.[82]
- Only three percent of Latinos support the term "Latinx",[83] a term that was popular among Martha's Vineyardians.

- The Minneapolis Teachers Union now requires schools to lay off or rehire employees based on race.[84] Despite a more garish tone, this sounds like affirmative action that society long ago negotiated as a viable path. The Supreme Court is about to take this on. Cue the street protests in 3...2...1...

- The American Academy of Pediatrics discourages schools from sending kids with head lice home because of "significant stigma and stress." [85] Maybe it would help if the teachers quit calling them Bug Heads and making allusions to *Men in Black.*

- People of Color are now called People of the Global Majority.[86] The rest of us are now referred to as "minorities."

- I'm gonna touch a third rail that I swore I would never touch. There is a palpable rising anti-Semitism. I suspect it is arising from pro-Palestinian groups. Who knows. My point is that the media is showing evidence they will be hanging it on white supremacists. Take it with a grain of salt.

- Female prisoners in a New Jersey prison got knocked up by inmates identifying as women. Free room, board, and unlimited sex sounds better than life on the Streets of San Francisco.[87]

- Alec Baldwin shot one of his coworkers, which is more than the January 6 insurrectionists shot. We *all* know this because it obstructs senseless babbling about laptops. A picture shows that Alec owns a pillow embroidered with, "Shoot first ask questions afterward", available from MyPillow.com.

- BLM laundered millions into who the hell knows.[88,89] Some of it was traced to an expensive house for one of the founders.[90] It is said that every movement becomes a business and ends as a racket.

- A woman posting as "@libsoftiktok" rose to Twitter fame by simply posting some of the quirkier videos posted on TikTok—statements in their own words. I suspect fakes might be a popular sport now, much in the way that Penthouse Letters emanated from Harvard dorms. There is a wide-open niche for "@conservativesoftiktok". I would start with this hysterical crime scene video.[91] Until then, expect violent and well-funded counterattacks to continue unabated.

- Somebody compiled a montage of all the times Joe Rogan failed to discreetly use the euphemistic "N-word." [92] (I am not gonna swat *that* fly.) He survived the attacks and even got a $100 million offer to move to Rumble for unrestrained speech.[93] Progressives would never make such a mistake. Just yankin' your chain: Of course they did![94]

Matthew Rosenberg @
@AllMattNYT

Joe Rogan is what he is. We in the media might want to spend more time thinking about why so many people trust him instead of us.

3:36 PM · Jan 30, 2022

♡ 91.3K   ◯ Reply   🔗 Copy link

Read 9K replies

- Teachers at Oak Park and River Forest High School are being told to adjust their grades to account for "the skin color or ethnicity of its students."[95] The basic protocol will use paint chips from Ace Hardware, and economists will be called in for "seasonal adjustments." Speaking of which, Governor Newsom wants to give $223,000 in reparations to Californians with slave roots.[96] One could imagine people moving to California—the Land of Bad Ideas—albeit temporarily.
- The mayor of San Francisco announced a $6.5 million plan to end homelessness in the city, but only for gender non-conforming individuals.[97] Sadly, $6.5 million wouldn't even dent Peoria's homeless gender non-conforming problem.
- A middle school librarian in relentlessly newsworthy Loudoun County, VA defended pro-prostitution books, noting that many of the school's 11–13-year-old students

are sex workers.[98] The problem is deeper than y'all thought. That teacher is grounded in a harsh reality.

- Drag queen shows for kids were all the rage in 2022. They appear to concentrate on target-rich opportunities (schools), but even Pizza Hut got into the game.[99] The pizza connection again? Those drag queen shows for toddlers is some very sick shit.

- Speaking of pizza, Matt Taibbi released former Twitter CEO Jack Dorsey's private email address: Jack@0.pizza.[100] One could call this *faux pas* "Pizzagate." The "0" could be important.

> It seems like we are doing everything we can to break everything possible.
>
> — Jordan Peterson

- A UCLA anthropology professor scrubbed the last of the rational thinkers from academia, announcing, "I'm a professor, retiring at 62 because the Woke takeover of higher education has ruined academic life," referring to how the anthropology department at UCLA had mutated since the early 2000s.[101]

ROE v. WADE

The human population would probably be way less than a thousand, if ejaculation were not usually accompanied by an orgasm.

— Mokokoma Mokhonoana

NEWS FLASH: The Roe versus Wade decision that bypassed the need to codify the right to an abortion was overturned. I am pro-choice, with an admittedly vague dotted line that defines when the nugget of cells develops civil rights.

I understand why a truce is likely to be metastable at best. When does life begin? The devout pro-lifers think that life begins at "just the tip" or "a lurid wink" while the activist left push it out past the four trimesters. Those who have raised teenagers think the sixtieth trimester should be open for discussion.

I listened closely to a Lex Fridman interview of Ben Shapiro, giving one of the sharpest pro-life advocates a shot at converting me.[1] He did not, but Ben made interesting points, including that the only *bright-line* demarcation is at conception. It becomes increasingly blurry after that. I can accept that ambiguity. If you have strong, clear views on the topic, you can skip this part. I wrote it to see where it would go.

Jesus never once talked about abortion. Never once.

—Joe Scarborough[2] (@JoeMSNBC)

I think we can all agree Joe has never once said anything intelligent. Never once. Moving along, I am convinced of the claims that the court overstepped its jurisdiction to resolve a thorny social issue.[3,4] The court were social engineers for Roe v. Wade, just like they were being economists when they overrode the gold standard in 1933. (For an excellent discussion of the court's history and the evolution of the Constitution, check out the audio short course in the Great Courses Series, entitled "The Bill of Rights."[5])

I wonder if efforts to codify abortion when Democrats were in power failed to emerge due to complacency or more complex lurking issues. Abortion rights may be more bipartisan than politicians would lead us to believe because, as Michael Jordan would say,[6] daughters of Republicans get knocked up too.

> Claiming that it was nearly impossible to amend the Constitution, Progressives advocated that judges "interpret" the Constitutional limits out of the way ... When the people wanted the Constitution amended, it was amended. When the elites wanted the Constitution amended, but the people did not, that is called democracy.[7]
>
> — Thomas Sowell, former Marxist turned free-market economist

The states' rights argument, that the people of Mississippi might wish to live under a different moral code than Californians, has merit. The U.S. is said to already have abortion laws that are the most liberal in the world.[8] You may recall that a few years back, North Carolina activists were pushing for abortions up to birth (implicitly even later).[9]

I've heard claims that the choice of the life of the fetus or of the mom is specious; that is what C-sections are for. But I'm not a doctor, and there are most definitely life-threatening pregnancies. I can also imagine scenarios in which the docs look at a truly pathetic failed late-stage pregnancy that cannot possibly end well, and make the call.

But that was not what was being codified. We are assured that *nobody* would ever abort a perfectly viable child within minutes of crawling out of the birth canal, but the proposed statutes (North Carolina, for example) appeared not to preclude it.

I think activists were doing what activists do: taking the cause to the extreme. I could also imagine a newborn taking one look at the world and crawling right back up the birth canal. As a pro-choice advocate, if you make me draw the line at one of the two extremes—never, or up to birth—I view the latter as infanticide and would choose the former. Please don't make me choose.

> To the extent this betrayal of the confidences of the Court was intended to undermine the integrity of our operations, it will not succeed ... I have directed the Marshal of the Court to launch an investigation into the source of the leak.[10]
>
> — Chief Justice John G. Roberts. Jr.

Then there was the leak to the press, days before the decision was announced. Of course it was denounced by the court as inexcusable, but leaks serve a purpose. There are possible suspects, beyond the butler with the candlestick.

- An irate clerk: Mind you, clerks are not clerical, but rather elite lawyers heading off to spectacular careers.

- A left-leaning justice: That field narrows quickly. It could have been an attempt to motivate the court to back off. This seems improbable, given that there is no way that the court wasn't braced for the backlash anyway.

- A right-leaning justice: Fence-sitting justices could be pushed into making an ironic tough choice of kowtowing to the masses or defending the sanctity of the court. This is akin to blowing up a pipeline to end negotiations.

- Bipartisan justices: Anticipating the shit storm, a leak would burn off some steam before reality struck; fourteen days to flatten the mob.

- Dark forces: Maybe the court has already been swallowed by the Deep State and is stirring up discontent, like every other wanker in the upper echelon of power.[11] Catherine Austin Fitts suggested that British, Israeli, or U.S. intelligence leaked it. Is it about Roe, or is it yet another attempt to tear the country apart? (I do not subscribe to this model, although maybe out of self-preservation.)

Many bills with varying intent were set to trigger in the event of such a ruling. By example, Colorado immediately passed a bill allowing abortion up until birth.[12] Protesters did their analog of January 6, albeit less raucous, by protesting at the courthouse and at the justices' homes. I would argue the optics were bad, but that speech is a protected right by those in the mob's sights.

> [I]t is a prized American privilege to speak one's mind, although not always with perfect good taste, on all public institutions, and this opportunity is to be afforded for 'vigorous advocacy' no less than 'abstract discussion' ...In light of our "profound national commitment to the principle that debate

on public issues shall be uninhibited, robust, and wide-open, and that it may well include vehement, caustic, and sometimes unpleasantly sharp attacks on government and public officials".[13]

— The *New York Times* v. Sullivan

The craziness started right on cue. The circus-like atmosphere included Alexandria Ocasio-Cortez pretending to have been handcuffed as she was escorted away from the Supreme Court. (I still think she is not *that* stupid, and the handcuffs elicit fantasies at so many levels.) Politicians and real people—an important distinction—screaming thoughtless threats are also protected. Threats against the justices were left up on Twitter,[14] in staggering contrast to Twitter's handling of other hot-button issues. While threats break Twitter rules, they are a form of protected speech. The Supreme Court ruled that a threat against the life of President Johnson was free speech because it lacked credibility.[15] While the politicians have the right to pander, We the People ought to have the right to jam socks in their mouths.

I wonder how long we're going to have these institutions at the rate we're undermining them, and then I wonder when they're gone or they are destabilized, what we'll have as a country—and I don't think that the prospects are good if we continue to lose them.

— Clarence Thomas, Supreme Court Justice

The media played its role in the drama. The neo-Stalinist social media platform, YouTube, began removing misinformation about abortion (whatever that is) to ensure that the lively debate would be ill-informed.[16] Vivid clips of late-stage abortions were fine, for some reason.[17] A pro-choice Twitter feed (MeidasTouch) emerged and had a million followers and a blue checkmark before the week was over.[18] Bill Burr's hilarious anti-abortion routine using the theme of a half-baked cake ("It wasn't a cake yet but I was gonna eat that fuckin' cake") got a second wind.[19]

CNN met my expectations yet again by announcing that the biggest threat of the Roe v. Wade decision was "violence from far-right groups."[20] Yeah, that makes sense, said nobody.

Companies began offering all-expense paid trips to pro-abortion states in order to keep their employees off maternity leave.[21,22] Walmart's support[23] was inspired by the People of Walmart[24] website, which clearly illustrates that breeding is not always a good idea.

As an aside, I think both sides of the debate could, in theory, support tree tube tying, which would cut back on abortions and unwanted pregnancies—a pragmatic move in an overcrowded world. Neither, however, seems likely to support my alternative to eugenics.

While Rome burned, the Supreme Court continued to fiddle.

- It supported a high school football coach's First Amendment rights to pray at the fifty-yard line during football games; his payers could choose whether to join in.[25] Hard to envision a left-leaning court ruling this way.
- It torched a Texas law that tried to prevent social media platforms from de-platforming contributors for political reasons.[26] I would say the Court has not kept up with the digital era. There are likely to be some big decisions in our future.

- Judge Ketanji Brown Jackson was asked by Sen. Marsha Blackburn, "Can you provide a definition for the word 'woman'?" She responded, "I can't. Not in this context. I'm not a biologist." [27] I will unexpectedly take her side; an elite judge ought to see the complexity and the trap. If you have an XXY triple chromosome count, are you a woman or a man? Matt Walsh probably would be less charitable. (Just to creep out my fellow whackjobs, Judge Jackson cut her teeth on the Pizzagate case.[28]) The elite news outlet, Politico, captured the historic importance of Judge Brown's appointment.

In case you think the Court will now be less contentious, it is said to be heading for a ruling that could ban affirmative action. And with that, I will cease unifying the nation by pissing off everybody on both sides and move along.

TRUCKERS

> Talking with people who think differently is how we challenge ourselves ... challenging ourselves is how we grow.
>
> — Justin Trudeau

> Regardless of the fact that we are attacking your fundamental rights or limiting your fundamental rights and the Charter says that is wrong, we are still going to go ahead and do it. It's basically a loophole that allows the majority to override the fundamental rights of the minority.
>
> — Justin Trudeau, February 14, 2022

CANADA WAS SLOW to lighten up on vaccine mandates. Three million vaccine-hesitant holdouts lingered as the stats showed 90 percent of new COVID deaths in Canada were of vaccinated individuals.[1]

Mandated vaccines every nine months and for the foreseeable future[2] got the engines of the Canadian truckers revving. Deciding they had had enough of Trudeau's guff, the truckers took their rigs to Ottawa to protest the vaccine mandates and lockdowns. As the Freedom Convoy reached a record-shattering 70 kilometers (43 miles) in length, Canadians set off fireworks and celebrated from the bridge overpasses.

The Canadian Spring became the most civilized protest in history.[3] They cleaned and policed the streets. Rumors of Nazi or Confederate flags were utter nonsense. (Trudeau's film crew staged one photo-op before the truckers took it down.) To us Yanks to the south, this was a feel-good story. U.S. truckers began to mobilize for a convoy to Washington, D.C.,[4] but it was late and they smelled the January 6 playbook: detect the blitz, let them rush in, and throw a screen pass.

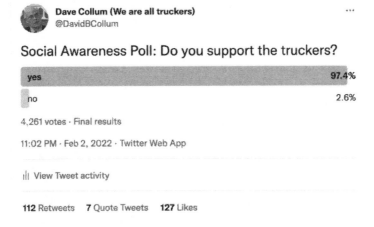

Dave Collum (We are all truckers)
@DavidBCollum

Social Awareness Poll: Do you support the truckers?

yes	97.4%
no	2.6%

4,261 votes · Final results

11:02 PM · Feb 2, 2022 · Twitter Web App

ili View Tweet activity

112 Retweets **7** Quote Tweets **127** Likes

Justin Trudeau ✓ @JustinTrudeau · 15h
⚑ Officiel du gouvernement - Canada
Today in the House, Members of Parliament unanimously condemned the antisemitism, Islamophobia, anti-Black racism, homophobia, and transphobia that we've seen on display in Ottawa over the past number of days. Together, let's keep working to make Canada more inclusive.

> What is driving this movement is a very small, organized group that is driven by an ideology to overthrow the government through whatever means they may wish to use.
>
> — Marco Mendicino, Canada's Public Safety Minister [5]

Taking a cue from the COVID authoritarians in Australia, Trudeau invoked the Emergency Measures Act (formerly known as the War Measures Act).[6] The move was opposed by the premiers of Alberta, Manitoba, Quebec, and Saskatchewan, but a WEF globalist pawn[7] does as he is told. Given that vaccine mandates were disappearing globally, what was at issue was not vaccines *per se* but the risk of a big win by the Deplorables. Truckers are global. *The State had to win.*

- They began arresting truckers.[8] The organizers of the "Freedom Convoy" were hit with onerous charges—not unlike the January 6 clampdown.[9]
- Chrystia Freeland, Deputy Prime Minister, authorized financial institutions "to temporarily cease providing financial services" and "review their relationships with anyone involved in the blockade."[10] She also claimed that the "temporary" financial oppressions to demonize the "violent extremists" were to become permanent, and that trucker's licenses would be suspended.[11] I return below to Permanent Bitch Face (PBF).

> Under the Emergencies Act, I've asked our solicitor and our city manager, "how can we keep the tow trucks and the campers and the vans and everything else that we've confiscated, and sell those pieces of equipment to help recoup some of the costs that our taxpayers are absorbing?"
>
> — Mayor of Ottawa

- Telephone and wireless services were shut down, forcing stores to accept cash, a commodity not easily obtained by the truckers.

- The Royal Canadian Mounted Police (RCMP) disabled trucks *pre-emptively*, in case they would be used for the protest.[12]
- Canadian broadcasters began lying about foreign actors backing the truckers.[13]
- Towing companies were required to begin towing trucks. Compliance was spotty.[14]

Justin Trudeau ✓
@JustinTrudeau
⚑ Officiel du gouvernement - Canada

When a government starts trying to cancel dissent or avoid dissent is when it's rapidly losing its moral authority to govern -Harper in 2005

12:40 p.m. · 23 May 12 · Twitter for iPad

769 Retweets **308** Quote Tweets **876** Likes

- Authorities threatened to euthanize the pet dogs that some of the truckers brought along, if the truckers were taken into custody and no other provisions were made.[15] I imagine volunteer rescues would have been legion. I would take in at least a dozen.
- Bank accounts of supporters and donors were shut down.[16]
- $20 million was raised for the truckers via GoFundMe and GoSendMe. An Ontario court froze GoFundMe, while

GoSendMe was hacked.[17] GoFuckYourselves requires no funds and is fully staffed.

> I think if you are a member of a pro-Trump movement who's donating hundreds of thousands of dollars and millions of dollars to this kind of thing, you ought to be worried.[18,19]
>
> — David Lametti, Canada's Justice Minister, threatening southern neighbors

- The communications director for the Ontario ministry donated $100 and was fired after being caught by a hack.[20]
- Declaring the truckers and their supporters to be terrorists got *no* backing from Canada's chief financial intelligence agency.[21]

WORLD
ECONOMIC
FORUM

Join us

Chrystia Freeland

Deputy Prime Minister and Minister of Finance, Office of
the Deputy Prime Minister of Canada

- Chrystia Freeland noted that, "The names of both individuals and entities as well as crypto wallets have been shared by the RCMP with financial institutions and accounts have been frozen and more accounts will be frozen." [22,23] PBF repulses me.

> Should the United States sanction Canada for human rights abuses?
>
> — Tom Fitton, president of Judicial Watch

Canadian authorities became what French Canadians call "douchebags". To understand why, you have to look under the hood of the leaders.

> The illusion of freedom will continue as long as it's profitable to continue the illusion. At the point where the illusion becomes too expensive to maintain, they will just take down the scenery, they will pull back the curtains, they will move the tables and chairs out of the way, and you will see the brick wall at the back of the theater.
>
> — Frank Zappa

Canada is filled with Ukrainians that populated the country after World War II, presumably some under a program akin to but much bigger than Operation Paperclip.[24]

Chrystia Freeland began her career as a Ukraine-based news correspondent, speaking fluent Ukrainian and Russian. Like a disturbing number of Canadian leaders,[25] she is a member of the WEF [26,27] and comes from a strong lineage of Ukrainian Nazis, beginning with a grandfather who was a Nazi propagandist.[28,29,30]

She is said to be a Banderite, which is the Ukrainian group that explicitly celebrates its Ukrainian Nazi past on the birthday of Stepan Bandera.[31] She supported the "Revolution of Dignity" in Kyiv—the Banderites' coup—and shepherded nearly $900 million to Ukraine in 2022 as part of a long history of supporting Ukraine.[32] Jim Rickards says she is in the queue— that is French Canadian for "in line"—to become Secretary General of NATO.

My opinion of NATO's leadership is clarified in the sections on the U.S.-Russia proxy war in Ukraine, but it is not a flattering story. Chrystia has the credentials to be a bad person.

Let's now talk about Trudeau, referred to as a "creepy fucking dictator" by Joe Rogan. I find him less dangerous than Freeland because he seems like an expendable twit. His roots go back to his legal father, former Canadian Prime Minister Pierre Trudeau. Pierre had profound ties to Mao and Castro, back when none of the cool kids supported those guys.[33]

> The level of admiration I actually have for China because their basic dictatorship is allowing them to actually turn their economy around on a dime and to say that we need to go green fast, invest in solar.
>
> —Justin Trudeau

The acorn may not have fallen far from the tree.

Or did it? The internet is filled with rumors that Justin's mother was a free-sex hippy. On the next page are two pictures of the Trudeaus with Castro. In the first, that is an unusually adoring look on Margaret Trudeau's face.

I learned a general rule in college: A hand on the back is tight on the personal space, but vague. A hand on the chest means you are gonna score.

I now ask what the internet has been asking for years.[34] Does Justin look like Pierre, and did Fidel get lucky?

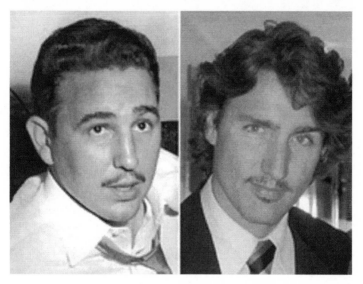

No more shits and giggles. I made a deadly serious case in my 2021 YIR that we are witnessing a rising (and potentially unstoppable) global authoritarianism.[35] Canada showed its fangs against the truckers. They had to keep the truckers in check because a global trucker uprising could lead to a Global Spring, which could become an unstoppable counterattack on the elites. The Road to Ukraine is not just about war; Western leaders are looking increasingly dangerous even at home.

PATRIOT FRONT

That is the 101st Airborne!

— Joe Rogan

THE PATRIOT FRONT is a funny story with a dark interior. It is a group of so-called white supremacists who march around covered in masks (leaders aside). They are a dapper group of young men who lack the paunches that you might expect to see in a MAGA militia, and are articulate.[1] They march in step, with military flair.[2] Their shields are all the same, and suspiciously similar to those in pictures from Ukraine. Early on they arrived in SUVs with deeply tinted windows and taped-over license plates, but later switched to U-Haul trucks. Strange videos show cops helping direct traffic while they load a truck.

On a fateful day in June 2022, Patriot Front members converged from across the country to cause trouble at an LGBTQ pride event in Coeur d'Alene, Idaho (population 50,000). It seems an odd target and an irrelevant venue on which to spend all that money. No BLM or Antifa, but Gay Pride? An "anonymous tip" alerted the police, and they were arrested for "spooning in a U-Haul," which was the only crime committed up to that moment.

A "conspiracy to riot" charge seems like a tough sell *before* the riot.[3] Is this a pre-crime? It also seems odd that the FBI didn't already have a bead on them.

The arrest was absurd. Their shoes all have the same soles: standard issue? They were handcuffed with zip ties, without removing their masks, a megaphone, or even their backpacks. I guess the cops weren't worried about concealed weapons or pipe bombs.

A Federal agent tore that apart, noting that *anything* posing a risk would be taken immediately and that it is entirely "stupid bullshit".[4] Another noted that you *never* leave suspects on their knees; it is too easy to get on your feet and run.[5] Others have also had quite a hoot over the whole affair.[6,7]

Take a look at their mug shots (on the next page). Do you notice anything odd? Twenty-one white supremacists, and not a single one has neck or facial tattoos.

Let's entertain the obvious theory that they are Feds. Why are they doing this? How is stirring up racial hatred not some sort of treason in this context? (I don't give the Feds a free speech pass on this one.) Since these guys signed up to protect the nation, how are they not repulsed by their role in undermining the fabric of society? Maybe they just work for the DNC.

I have only scratched the surface, and had dismissed white supremacists as somewhere between irrelevant and urban legend. In one of the strangest and most thoroughly made connections, these guys have been tied to the CIA and the Azov Battalion in Ukraine, part of the global Azov movement that includes the tiki torchers in Charlottesville that caused The Donald so much trouble.[8] There is nothing humorous about this Azov movement, which is increasingly looking like a worldwide problem, with Ukraine as a training ground. All roads lead to Ukraine.

UVALDE AND OTHER SHOOTINGS

> In the past 48 hrs, the USA horrifically lost 34 people to mass shootings. On average, across any 48 hrs, we also lose ... 500 to medical errors 300 to the Flu, 250 to Suicide, 200 to Car Accidents, and 40 to Homicide via Handguns. Often our emotions respond more to spectacle than to data.
>
> — Neil deGrasse Tyson (@neiltyson), world-renowned voice of physics

> As we grieve the children of Uvalde today, we should take time to recognize that two years have passed since the murder of George Floyd under the knee of a police officer. His killing stays with us all to this day, especially those who loved him.[1]
>
> — Barack Obama, former POTUS, pandering and getting guff for it

CONTRARY TO POPULAR OPINION, the U.S. is not the world leader in mass killings.[2] In the U.S., rifles kill fewer people than fists or knives.[3]

I am unclear when my interest in mass shootings morphed from morbid rubber-necking to distrust. It could have been the Florida nightclub shooting, where I kept seeing the same guy with a screwy hat in every scene in the mainstream media. There is, however, something going on here.

Comparing Annual Death Rate from Mass Public Shootings (Comparing European Countries to US and Canada From January 2009 to December 2015)

Rank	Country	Death Rate per million people from Mass Public Shootings from 2009 through 2015
1	Norway	1.888
2	Serbia	0.381
3	France	0.347
4	Macedonia	0.337
5	Albania	0.206
6	Slovakia	0.185
7	Switzerland	0.142
8	Finland	0.132
9	Belgium	0.128
10	Czech Republic	0.123
11	US	0.089
12	Austria	0.068
13	Netherlands	0.051
14	Canada	0.032
15	England	0.027
16	Germany	0.023
17	Russia	0.012
18	Italy	0.009

I was on a panel discussion this year in front of 500 investors. I was asked to name one conspiracy, not defend it, and take questions from the audience. My response: Many if not most of the mass shootings are sovereign-backed.

The shootings follow a similar protocol. Witnesses on the scene allude to multiple shooters, with the plot then distilling within 24 hours to one drug-addled teenager. After the body count, the kid is getting sentenced in court, never to be seen again—no digging for an explanation. The missing hard drives are problematic. Alex Jones discovered that chasing such stories to the extreme can be very expensive.

He is not the first mass shooter to destroy or hide digital clues. In 2007, [the] Virginia Tech shooter ... took the step of removing the hard drive of his computer and disposing of his cell phone shortly before the massacre ... The 2008 Northern Illinois [University] shooter, Steven Kazmierczak, removed the SIM card from his phone and the hard drive from his laptop, and neither was recovered ... In 2012, Sandy Hook shooter Adam Lanza had removed the hard drive from his computer and smashed it with a hammer or screwdriver.[4]

— ABC News (now scrubbed, but I read it)

This rogue's gallery of shooters looks like the senior class in the MK Ultra School for Wayward Boys.[5]

The Rosetta Stone for me is the 2017 Las Vegas shooting, in which over 500 concertgoers were shot and fifty died at the hand of Stephen Paddock, high up in the Mandalay Bay Casino. It was the largest domestic killing in the U.S. since Gettysburg. When was the last time you heard it mentioned? Why does the anti-gun lobby not use it as their rallying cry?

I wrote over a dozen pages pointing out countless absurdities in the plot[6] and will not revisit that story in depth, only add a couple of updates.

A documentary emerged,[7,8,9] or what I call an "answer key" to check how I did. *You really should watch it.* There is *nothing* about this narrative that holds water. This is not a plot with kinks in it, but a story in which nothing holds up to scrutiny. It was what is called a psyop (psychological operation) by sovereign State actors.

One of the most interesting theories to emerge is that it was cover for a State-sponsored assassination of Saudi Prince Al Waleed bin Talal,[10] but I will leave that for Alex to ponder.

Two characters played prominent parts in my awakening. First was Sheriff Lombardo of Clark County, whose story morphed from it being "physically impossible" for one shooter to have fired that many rounds to "one shooter" overnight. Mike Cronk, a hick from Alaska, kept getting interviewed over and over while his absurdly implausible story drifted. He even participated in a staged (faked) visit to his friend at the hospital. He was eventually labeled by others as a "crisis actor," which brought in more fact-checkers than Alaskan mountain men normally warrant.

Well, as of November 2022, they are now Governor Lombardo and State Senator Cronk. They played their parts. I may be nuts, but am not alone.

After a hiatus in shootings to make room for COVID, January 6, and Ukraine, there were a couple more. One heartwarming story was when a 22-year-old named Elisjsha Dicken cut short a mall massacre, with seven shots out of eight hitting the psycho from forty paces.[11] Young Wyatt Earp now has his own clothing line, a lifetime collection of memes, and a full dance card.

Elisjsha Dicken

Social Awareness Poll: Asking for a friend.

Thesis — The youthful mass murderers are troubled teens who have been befriended and manipulated by pros (State-sponsored psyops.) The odds of this are...

zero. WTF you thinking?	13.4%
Low but non-zero...	37.3%
disturbingly high	36%
high	13.3%

1,515 votes · Final results

11:16 PM · May 26, 2022

This is all heading somewhere. The headliner was the shooting in Uvalde, Texas. In June of 2022 an 18-year-old named Salvador Ramos slaughtered nineteen kids and two adults in an elementary school while the cops stood by and did nothing. Parents (some armed) trying to save their kids were pushed back with pepper spray and restrained with handcuffs. Seventy-seven minutes of carnage ensued before an off-duty Border Patrol officer shot and killed Ramos.

The cops had been trained only months earlier [12] and had installed expensive risk assessment tools.[13] Their profound lack of response has been blamed on incompetence, cowardice, and bureaucratic ossification resulting from anti-cop movements, rendering individuals unable to act outside strict, formulaic protocols. Videos show cops relentlessly retreating [14] and performing meme-generating activities, with one cop sanitizing his hands.

The official story is that the cops waited for the master key to be produced, in order to enter the school. *What?* It is no surprise that lawyers for the police tried not to release evidence.[15]

THEY WILL CLEANSE THEIR HANDS OF THEIR CONSCIOUSES WHILE YOU PAY THEM TO BE COWARDS.

There are problems with this story that bug me. Unlike the Las Vegas shooting, where I think the craziness is so easy to document that it dominates the story, I do not have the smoking gun. But if sovereign actors are involved in even some of the mass shootings, we have to stay on this plot. Do it for the children. I warn you, there is no punchline here. Just concerns, presented in no particular order.

- The incompetence and cowardice models do not work for me. Most of those cops were dads. I imagine a few were ex-military. *None* ran in? The formal training says that once there is a shooting, you get to the shooter. Period.[16] I would have said that if you picked twenty guys out of the phonebook randomly, at least some of them would have responded to the primal screams in their head, yelling, "Kids are dying; let's get in there now." Recall the flight that went down over Shanksville, PA?
- Tucker Carlson went all-in on Las Vegas, and asked some analogous thorny questions about Uvalde too.[17]
- Ramos was from an impoverished family yet had $4,000 worth of guns and ammo.
- Ramos was shooting up Uvalde fifteen minutes before entering the school.
- There is debris that, as demonstrated by Alex Jones, should be left alone. But it is out there, for the most curious.[18,19]
- A mother ran into the school to save her two children. She claimed the police were muzzling her and told a strangely inconsistent tale of the events.[20] She describes escaping, being detained in the school by the officers, begging them "for a vest", and then declaring there "was not one officer in the school."

- Uvalde has a population of 15,217. It is located in the Texas Hill Country, eighty miles west of San Antonio and fifty-four miles east of the Mexican border. Curious: 372 cops were said to be on the scene.
- Four years ago, two 14-year-olds in Uvalde were arrested for plotting to commit mass murder. Investigators said they were infatuated with the Columbine shootings. The plan was to do this *upon graduation*,[21,22] in June 2022, the month of the shooting. Neither kid was Ramos. The author of the articles *was* named Ramos, a common name in the region.
- Both the border guard who killed the shooter and the mom who saved the kids are heroes. Where did they go? What are their names? Why are they not famous, with tons of interviews?

The entire Uvalde school district police force was suspended five months later.[23] My school never had a district police force. The survivors have just filed a class-action lawsuit, which makes sense, although $27 billion is a reach.[24]

CLIMATE CHANGE

> And so, I hope President Putin will help us to stay on track with respect to what we need to do for the climate.
>
> — John Kerry, February 23, 2022

HAVING BANGED OUT DOZENS OF PAGES describing my transition from climate believer (but not a true believer) to climate denier (a true denier), I have come to terms with the climate change story and retain little interest.

Whether it is occurring or not, the dominant narrative is a mass movement playing into an estimated $150 trillion grift.[1] I'd love some of that action.

Here are just a few tidbits.

- 31,000 scientists signed a petition saying I am not the only nutjob denying the climate crisis.[2] Jordan Peterson did a real nice riff on it.[3]
- There are calls for the censorship of climate denial because the climate cultists are morons and demand shit like that.[4,5]
- Everything, from an increased number of hurricanes (there is no such increase[6]) to a pandemic of myocarditis (there is one of those) is attributed by the cult to climate change.
- Scientists trying to resurrect the woolly mammoth presumed we are Neanderthals when they claimed that mammoths would help climate change by packing down the snow.[7]

- The National Oceanographic and Atmospheric Administration (NOAA) suggested that pollution *decreases* the severity of hurricanes, which is funny, but I don't believe that either.[8]
- Sri Lanka bought into the story, racking up a near-perfect ESG score, higher than that of Sweden, in the old-fashioned way. They are now starving to death, and grumpy about it.[9]
- Germans want to hike the price of meat by 56 percent through a meat tax.[10] Food shortages this winter could solve that problem.
- Dutch farmers were told not to grow any food as we may be heading into the teeth of global "food insecurity," also known as "famine," owing to "nitrogen pollution."[11] Next up: oxygen pollution.
- U.S. authorities want $4–6 trillion per year to fight climate change.[12] The true believers are being grifted on a colossal scale. Saving the whales was successful and a *lot* cheaper.

I am sorry if I insulted you [*editor's note*: No, he is not.] but I do think some of you are what Eric Hoffer would call "true idiots." If you wish to talk about environmental destruction, resource depletion, and even overpopulation, I am all ears. I also *know* there are serious climate scientists out there. It is time for y'all to speak up or get tarred with my big brush.

Here is my rule of thumb: anyone mentioning climate change in a non-scientific article has no clue what he or she is talking about.

Daily Mail U.K. ✓
@DailyMailUK

Climate change is making migraines, strokes and DEMENTIA more severe and common, review claims

NINA JANKOWICZ

MY EXPECTATION for the Biden administration was low, but not zero. I thought he would pivot to the center and be a generic president. It is not a partisan thing; almost all of my friends are Democrats and I had no serious gripes about Obama.

But I believe Biden has been a wretched president. His personal screwups are legion—I have pages of notes and anecdotes—but somehow, chronicling them doesn't interest me. Somebody filled his administration with total misfits.

But I refuse to give him a pass just because he is demented. I think he is hair-sniffing perv, a corrupt-to-the-core swindler, a compulsive liar, and treasonous in his international dealings with foreign countries. Those making major decisions for him—certainly not Harris, and in my opinion not Obama either—appear to be hell-bent on destroying the country. I am biased; profoundly so at this point.

> Unless you turn back now and disband this Orwellian Disinformation Governance Board immediately, the undersigned will have no choice but to consider judicial remedies to protect the rights of their citizens.[1]
>
> — Letter from twenty State Attorneys General

I want to zoom in on one appointment in particular, that of Nina Jankowicz, because her role is *very* interesting to me. She was appointed head of a new "Disinformation Governance Board" which came to be called the Ministry of Truth, located within the Department of Homeland Security. That such an

Orwellian concept was put into practice underscores my disdain—no, my hatred—for the neo-Stalinists who have been pushing the nation to the brink.

Nina, however, is a quirky individual. She introduced herself to the world by singing Mary Poppins tunes about the evils of Donald Trump.[2,3]

Critical race theory has become one of those hot-button issues that the Republicans and other disinformers, who are engaged in disinformation for profit, frankly ... have seized on.

— Nina Jankowicz, Disinformation Governance Board

Her neo-Stalinist leanings, however, are anything but benign. She expressed the need to intervene (edit and moderate) in social media.[4] In her alternative reality, social media (prior to Elon Musk's purchase) was censoring the political left, which was ridiculous at the time and demonstrably false now with the release of the Twitter documents.[5]

She believes government should set minimum speech standards.

Other items of interest: banning misogyny, referring to "freedom of expression and fairy dust," algos that would "allow us to get around some of the free speech concerns,"[6] and that free speech makes her "shudder".[7]

Despite the *New York Times'* spin, the plot takes several odd turns. The decidedly left-leaning *The Nation* ran an exposé on Nina, accusing their peers of faltering due diligence.[8] Our insufferable Vaudevillian has a dark side. Beginning in college, she worked with StopFake, a government-funded propaganda machine charged with combating Kremlin lies. StopFake was pivotal in sanitizing violent Ukrainian neo-Nazi groups. It partners with Facebook fact-checkers to censor news. It was founded in 2014, during Ukraine's CIA-led coup that brought a U.S.-backed government to power. It was sold as a grass-roots antagonist to Russian propaganda. It even has George Soros's Open Society Foundations backing to make the story juicy. Jankowicz was in Ukraine as a Fulbright Clinton Public Policy Fellow.

Years before Jankowicz's "warm portrayal of volunteer battalions," *The Nation* had described their "'ISIS-style' War Crimes." The article is a must-read to understand both Nina, Ukraine, and the Ukrainian Azov Battalion. And, if that is not weird enough, she just satisfied federal law by registering as a foreign agent.[9] All roads lead to Ukraine.

And with all those foreshadowings, let's actually look at what the hell happened in Ukraine in Part 2 of the 2022 Year in Review.

PART TWO

THE WAR IN UKRAINE

> Hello darkness, my old friend
> I've come to talk with you again
>
> — Simon and Garfunkel, *The Sound of Silence*

> The decision of one man to launch a wholly
> unjustified and brutal invasion of Iraq ... I mean of
> Ukraine ...[1]
>
> — former President G. W. Bush, Freudian slipping

WE ARE ON THE CUSP of WW III, which could become the most inclusive war in history, with world leaders who seem incapable of orchestrating a decisive paintball attack.

Like so many, I rely on geopolitical events to learn about politics and geography. Task #1: figure out where Ukraine is located on a map. I stumbled upon this top-secret Pentagon strategy map.

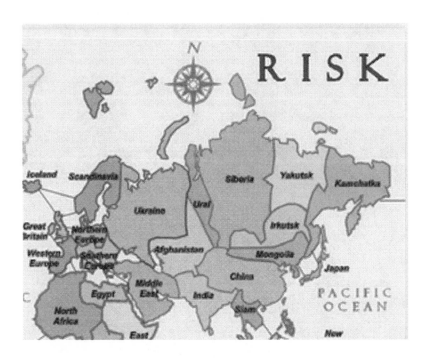

Oh my God. They have already removed Russia!

Task #2: resolve spelling and grammar issues. Is it Ukraine or The Ukraine; Odesa or Odessa; Kiev or Kyiv; Zelensky or Zelenskiy or Zelenskyy; Donbas or Donbass; and Dumbass or Biden?

First disclaimer: I have no chance of understanding a border war in or near the Baltics. I take solace in that y'all are in the same boat. I am grand theorizing—creating big narratives for a hopelessly complex topic. I am describing The World According to Dave. I am layers into the onion but doubtlessly layers away from truths, because I am fishing shit off the internet about a war said by the legendary journalist John Pilger and filmmaker Oliver Stone to be the most propaganda-slathered war in their lifetimes.[2,3]

My immutable rule of thumb: if their lips are moving, they are lying.

> War cannot be reduced to distinction between good guys and bad guys.[4]
>
> — Pope Francis

We can all agree that the list of victims in this war is non-statistically populated by Ukrainians. They are dying, and their world is being upended. If, however, you think that this is a simple story about good versus evil, you need a CT scan.

Here I am talking especially to devout members of the Sanctimony-Industrial Complex—Eric Hoffer's fanatical True Believers—who will take any opportunity to become a part of a grand movement in order to elevate their lives by signaling their virtue.

I was on a Zoom call with a member of the clergy in which he said, "It is Putin's fault because Putin attacked." I curtly told that punk-ass zealot—quite an impressive one, actually—that "If I have some guy in my face, and it is clear that this is not going to resolve well, my immediate goal becomes finding a way to land the first punch, to ensure there is no second punch." (I *did* say that.) Months later I discovered that I had inadvertently paraphrased Putin.

If you think Putin is, by definition, wrong because he attacked first, you have neither read much nor thought very deeply about the Ukraine conflict or the origins of wars.

> We could have hit Saudi Arabia—it was part of that bubble—could have hit Pakistan. We hit Iraq because we could.[5]
>
> — Thomas Friedman, author and The Great Pontificator

When caught in a conversation with somebody who is certain about Russia being the sole instigator, I resort to moral equivalency and ask, "Which sovereign state has bombed more countries and killed more people over the last two decades: the U.S. or Russia?" The U.S. has intervened militarily 251 times since 1991.[6] The Obama administration bombed seven Muslim countries. Bush Jr. killed upwards of a million Iraqis. Which of those countries attacked us? (Hint: none.)

The U.S. conducted three consecutive days of airstrikes in Syria in 2022. The Pentagon said, "These strikes are a message to Tehran."[7,8] That's so odd, because I didn't realize that Tehran is in Syria. Or did we bomb one country to send a message to another country?

I can hear somebody saying, "But ... but ... they were dangerous because ..." Oh, shut the fuck up and go hum a few bars of *Crimea River*, Justin.[9] That does not give us the right to bomb them back to the Stone Age. There are many countries with nukes that we don't bomb.

Here are Leslie Stahl and Secretary of State Madeleine Albright in 1996, comparing notes on the Iraq War.[10]

> *Stahl:* We have heard that a half million [Iraqi] children have died. I mean, that's more children than died in Hiroshima. And, you know, is the price worth it?
>
> *Albright:* I think this is a very hard choice, but the price—we think the price is worth it.

You're right, Madeleine. Nobody gives a shit about brown people, anyway; Chris Hedges sarcastically calls them "bad victims," unworthy of our empathy. A montage was prepared, of virtuous members of the U.S. press expressing why we *should* care about Ukrainians, unlike other victims—*they are like us!* [11]

By the way, back when Madeleine was green-lighting the slaughter of children, does anyone remember the Western press airing footage of those atrocities? Any photos of the half-million bloated and dismembered carcasses of children? Agree with her if you like, but *statistically speaking*, it's the U.S. leaders who should be taken to The Hague for crimes against humanity.

> The greatest crime since World War II has been U.S. foreign policy.
>
> — Ramsey Clark, former U.S. Attorney General

So here is my advice to the sanctimonious: drop the holier-than-thou 'tude when talking about this war. While you are at it, ponder why y'all justified punishing musicians and conductors,[12,13] professional athletes,[14] or just wealthy people [15,16,17] simply because they have Roosky heritage. Why not lock them in barracks for the duration of the war, like the Japanese Americans? Bombing a Russian cultural center in Paris seems a tad excessive.[18]

Facebook and Instagram adjusted their hate speech policies to allow users to incite violence against Russians and Russian soldiers, and turned off the spigot for anything that smacked of being pro-Russia.[19]

All this should seem a little jingoistic, even to the most sanctimonious. As an aside, are the neo-Marxists on college campuses monitoring Russian students' well-being, or are they concerned only about Ukrainians?

> As a result of the Russian invasion of Ukraine, we have temporarily made allowances for forms of political expression that would normally violate our rules like violent speech such as "death to the Russian invaders." [20]
>
> — Facebook

Take a peek at this 2022 documentary [21] about a very quirky 1985 film entitled "Come and See," [22] illustrating Russia's experience of the horrors of war. While watching our elite try to bend Russians to our will at the expense of the Ukrainians, don't forget that *nobody* knows how to suffer like a Russian. Then lighten it up with this British comedy skit that asks the rhetorical question, "How do we know we are not the baddies?" [23]

> The notion that a political leader, or anyone for that matter, is entirely bad or good, is puerile. The same consideration can be given to nation-states, political systems or even models of world order. The character of a human being, a nation or a system of global governance is better judged by their or its totality of actions. [24]
>
> — Iain Davis, independent investigative journalist

Wars are never simple. Recall that we got into the 2003 Iraq War due to fake stories about babies being stabbed in incubators, [25] bullshit evidence of weapons of mass destruction (which, I should reiterate, does *not* give us the right to bomb a country), and intel from a deep source named "Curveball" who would say anything in exchange for a few of the C-notes being shipped to Fallujah on pallets by the CIA.[26]

Or maybe go back further and consider:

- the U.S. baiting Germany to sink the arms-laden *Lusitania*, in order to enter WW I;[27]
- the *fully provoked* attack by Japan through a door left wide open at Pearl Harbor, in order to enter WW II;[28]
- the Gulf of Tonkin fiasco, to get us into Vietnam;[29]
- the Gulf War, a trap set by our State Department, while ostensibly being about liberating Kuwaitis from the evil Saddam Hussein.[30]

> We have no opinion on your Arab–Arab conflicts, such as your dispute with Kuwait. Secretary [of State James] Baker has directed me to emphasize the instruction, first given to Iraq in the 1960s, that the Kuwait issue is not associated with America.[31]
>
> — April Glaspie, U.S. ambassador, setting the trap on Saddam to invade Kuwait

SOURCES

To hear the accepted War in Ukraine narrative, turn on CNN or MSNBC. My strategy was to examine the events that *pre-date* the Drums of War. After the war began, the media coverage was bullshit (and turtles) all the way down.

In the following sections I'll talk about my sources and describe the key players in this drama. We'll then wander through some contemporary events that run counter to the mainstream narrative.

Just to reiterate: from a dead cold start, there is no way I have the entire, correct story. I can, however, offer up pieces of a huge jigsaw puzzle that seem to match. I identify as a Reagan Republican, not some commie dog, although I appear to be playing one on the internet. Woof. I am challenging conventional wisdom *because* I wish to fulfill our dreams of being the good guys.

Dave "Free Rudy" Collum @DavidBCollum · Jun 25
A little perspective...

BEFORE UKRAINE CRISIS	AFTER UKRAINE CRISIS
The Guardian	**The Guardian**
"Welcome to Ukraine, the most CORRUPT nation in Europe"	"The fight for Ukraine is a fight for liberal IDEALS"
REUTERS	REUTERS
"Ukraine's neo-NAZI problem"	"For foreign fighters, Ukraine offers purpose, camaraderie and a CAUSE"
Vox	CNN
"A Ukrainian comedian-turned-president is embroiled in Trump's impeachment MESS"	"Ukrainians are giving two LESSONS in democracy that Americans have forgotten"
NEWEUROPE	The Washington Post
"Ukrainian president's rule becomes increasingly corrupt, AUTHORITARIAN"	"Zelensky: The TV president turned war HERO"

○ 29   ⟲ 794   ♡ 1,896   ⬆   ⅲ

While trying to sort out such complex stories, I avoid reading books. I want to assemble a narrative rather than reiterate somebody else's. Of course, even the pieces of the puzzle have embedded narratives and may be laced with propaganda. It is my compromise.

But I broke my "no books" rule this time by reading *The Rise and Reign of Vladimir Putin* by Steven Myers,[1] recommended by America's favorite Roosky, Lex Fridman. I must admit it seemed remarkably balanced and unbiased, until the moment Putin was elected President. From that page on,

Myers had *nothing* favorable to say—not one positive word. It was as though a new author took control, or aggressive editing began, or the zebra changed the color of his stripes at that moment.

I am still looking for a book that is neither pro- nor anti-Putin. A six-part psychoanalysis of him was overconfidently overstated and biased to the core, but had some interesting logic.[2]

Useful source materials include documentaries such as "Ukrainian Agony,"[3] "Ukraine—Masks of the Revolution,"[4] and especially Oliver Stone's "Ukraine on Fire" (2016)[5] and his discussion of Putin with Lex Fridman.[6] I also binge-watched every Putin interview and speech I could find, including Stone's multi-part interview.[7,8,9]

Precious few pundits are willing to speak out against NATO. Here are capsule sketches of notable allies—comrades, if you will—advocating their asses off.

> What's going on here is that the West is leading Ukraine down the primrose path, and the end result is that Ukraine is going to get wrecked.
>
> —John Mearsheimer, 2015

John Mearsheimer graduated from West Point, got his PhD at Cornell, and is on the faculty at the University of Chicago. He has been *the* most outspoken detractor of NATO for over a decade, asserting its policies are driving us toward World War III.[10,11,12,13,14,15,16] He passed along a Munk Debate to me, in which he and Steve Walt (Harvard Kennedy School) took on Michael McFaul (former Ambassador to Russia) and Radosław Sikorski (member of the European Parliament and former Polish Minister of Defense), along with some choice private opinions of his opponents' tactics and attitudes.[17] I will kiss-and-tell one line from that email: "It is impossible to slow this train down save for nuclear use." Mearsheimer laments that democracies waging distant wars are consistently the biggest liars. "That, in a nutshell, is the United States." Meanwhile, the media no longer searches for truth, having become an administrative state—a pawn of the Deep State.

> *Jeff Sachs (at the Athens Democracy Forum):* The most violent country in the world since 1950 has been the United States.
>
> *Moderator, interrupting:* Jeffrey ... Let's ... Jeffrey: Stop now. Let's ... Let's ... Jeffrey, I'm ... I'm ... I'm your moderator, and it's enough.
>
> *Jeffrey:* OK. I'm done [applause and laughter].[18,19]

Jeffrey Sachs is an elite economist from Columbia University who was an advisor to many of the Warsaw Pact nations in the post-Soviet Union world.[20,21,22,23,24,25] He may not always be right, but he calls balls and strikes and says he cannot even get op-eds published now.

> This war and suffering could have easily been avoided if Biden Admin/NATO had simply acknowledged Russia's legitimate security concerns regarding Ukraine's becoming a member of NATO, which would mean U.S./NATO forces right on Russia's border.
>
> — Tulsi Gabbard

Tulsi Gabbard, former Democratic Congresswoman from Hawaii, recently estranged from the DNC, has a military background and has consistently taken an anti-war stance. She argues firm to the notion that NATO was the proximate trigger and could have prevented the war.[26,27] (Coda: I suspect her estrangement from the DNC might have been purchased with a promise to be a VP running mate in 2024. We shall see. I have also called out Svante Myrick as a DNC-derived presidential candidate several decades from now. We shall see about that, too.)

> One of the first lessons of objectivity is to slow things down to make sure that fact is not obscured by emotion.
>
> — Scott Ritter

Scott Ritter is a former Marine Corps intelligence officer who provides technical analysis of the war that conflicts with CNN's.[28,29,30,31,32,33] He first came under the spotlight testifying in front of an irate Joe Biden, who spurned Scott's intel indicating that there were no weapons of mass destruction in Iraq.[34] Mearsheimer referred to Scott's Gulf War analyses as "so knowledgeable."[35] Although his resume has some scuff marks related to inappropriate sexual conduct,[36] his sparring with the Deep State renders such blemishes highly suspect, and irrelevant anyway. Ritter has proven himself particularly prescient by predicting Russia's military strategy in Ukraine, events that were later interpreted differently in the mainstream media when they played out as described.

> NATO had ample opportunity for peace but deliberately chose war. The U.S. realized that, with

> Russia's back to the wall, it would have no choice but to attack.
>
> — Richard Black

Colonel Richard Black served 31 years in the U.S. Marine Corps and later served in the Virginia State Senate. He does *not* get smeared on Wikipedia.[37] He views the Ukraine war as a resource grab of Ukraine *and* Russia by the U.S., under the cover of NATO. In 2022 he wrote an open letter to Congress warning of the mounting risks of military conflict that began in 2014.[38,39,40] He decried the lure of "war profits even if it means gambling the lives of hundreds of millions of people across the globe."

> There's this attempt to destroy Russia. We've decided to make it this blood-enemy that has to be eliminated because it refuses to march down the path that Europe has.
>
> — Colonel Douglas Macgregor

Colonel Douglas Macgregor is a highly decorated Gulf War veteran. He is known as innovative, with unconventional thinking.[41] His views on the U.S. role in the Middle East are hawkish. In brutally direct language, he supports Russia's claims about the Donbas region going back to 2014.[42,43,44,45] The Senate blocked his nomination as ambassador to Germany, and he narrowly missed an appointment as National Security Advisor.

> War propaganda stimulates the most powerful aspects of our psyche, our subconscious, our

> instinctive drives ... The more unity that emerges in support of an overarching moral narrative, the more difficult it becomes for anyone to critically evaluate it ... When critical faculties are deliberately turned off based on a belief that absolute moral certainty has been attained, the parts of our brain armed with the capacity of reason are disabled.[46]

> — Glenn Greenwald, Substack writer, most famous for his Snowden Tapes

Other voices dissenting against the prevailing narrative include off-Broadway journalists such as Scott Horton,[47] Ron Paul,[48] Max Blumenthal,[49] Aaron Mate,[50,51,52,53] Glenn Greenwald,[54,55] Nigel Farage,[56] Pope Francis,[57,58] Swiss Policy Research,[59] Chris Hedges,[60] European Union MEP Clare Daly,[61,62] Tucker Carlson,[63,64] former CIA analyst Ray McGovern,[65] former CIA analyst Jacques Baud,[66,67,68] journalist John Pilger,[69] Oliver Stone,[70] The Last American Vagabond,[71,72] Gonzalo Lira, on the ground in Ukraine,[73,74] Whitney Webb,[75] Tom Luongo,[76] Matt Taibbi,[77] pro-Soviet journalist Vladimir Pozner,[78] Substack blogger Kanekoa,[79] blogger Will Schryver (@imetatronink),[80] and even Jordan Peterson.[81]

THE PLAYERS

Four players are central to my version of this drama: Vladimir Putin, Volodymyr Zelensky, the North Atlantic Treaty Organization (NATO), and the Azov Battalion.

Before plowing into the swamp, I've got to confess that for a number of years now I have found myself sympathetic to Putin. He's no snowflake, but his moves on the global chessboard and role in Russian affairs seem decidedly logical relative to ours; he is tactically maxed out.

— me, in my 2017 Year in Review

Vladimir Putin is an enigmatic figure who I mentioned in 2014, after the Ukrainian coup, highlighting Mearsheimer's warnings;[1] in 2015, in light of Syria and a brief shutdown of Russian natural gas;[2] in 2016, about the Drums of War becoming audible;[3] in 2017, trying to unscramble the Steele dossier and Russian collusion farce;[4] and in 2018, while analyzing the farcical stories about the Skripal poisoning and my efforts to cause an international incident by calling the British liars on *Russia Today*.[5]

I have the disadvantage of knowing nothing about Russia, especially compared to those who have spent time in the region. Or maybe that's an advantage—a friend of mine with Ukrainian ties loses his shit when talking about the subject—but if so it is a marginal advantage.

I find the West's tendency to blame Putin for everything imaginable, including an increasing number of clearly self-inflicted wounds, to be deeply troubling and dangerous.

Trump's strongest campaign plank in 2016 was, for me, his desire to "get along with the Russians." Of course, the Deep State put a lid on that with fake Russian collusion stories.

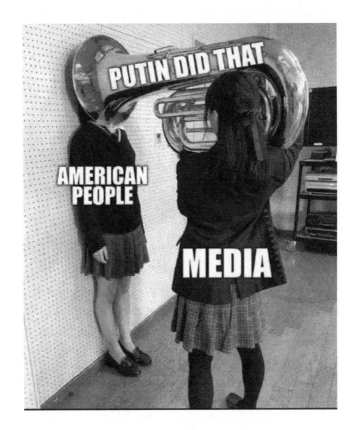

Putin is as inscrutable as you would expect an ex-KGB agent and current leader of Russia to be. My opinion of the man is largely aligned with that of Oliver Stone in his interview with Lex Fridman.[6]

Here are some opinions of Putin masquerading as declarative statements.

- Putin is probably scarred by his tough Russian upbringing, leaving him with inadequate compassion. By Western standards, he would be considered a sociopath.[7] Although often called a narcissist, that seems too simple. I have no doubt that more than a few who crossed him regretted it, but neither do I doubt that Western media distortions are profound.

- He is a Russian nationalist. While his geopolitical tactics are not soft-touch, I find claims that he is attempting to reassemble the Soviet Union to be far-fetched propaganda. His famous lamenting of the collapse of the Soviet Union is usually taken out of context. He was troubled by the post-collapse chaos, which could have been avoided. I see a loose analogy with the period in Britannia following the Roman withdrawal.

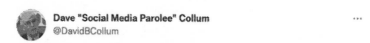

Dave "Social Media Parolee" Collum
@DavidBCollum

Social Awareness Poll: Who do you think cares most about the well being of their home country?

Putin	71.7%
Trudeau	1.3%
Biden	3.1%
Zelenskyy	23.8%

2,500 votes · Final results

10:54 AM · Apr 22, 2022 · Twitter Web App

ıli View Tweet analytics

31 Retweets **4** Quote Tweets **58** Likes

- To Putin, loyalty is everything. It undoubtedly shuts down what Westerners might consider to be constructive open debate. The part missed by many is that in his younger years, as a subordinate, he offered the same fealty that he expects today. It was central to his rise to power.

- Putin's unflinching directness is brutally refreshing in a world with more waffles than an IHOP. In his interviews he shows little or no evasiveness.

- His gravitas dwarfs that of Western leaders, including Biden, Trudeau, and Macron. (I'm withholding judgment on Italy's decidedly spunky Meloni.) It is a low bar to hurdle, but gravitas is a minimum requirement if one wishes to rise in Russia. Pundits confounded by his domestic popularity should ask themselves why his image in the West is not so shabby either, despite their best efforts.

- He is not a madman, although rumors of recent mental demise lack hard data to support or refute them. Contemporary analyses of his physical and mental health are likely to be so tainted by the intelligence agencies as to be worthless. Judge him by his interviews.

- Some analyses paint Vlad as a strict rule follower.[8] By example, a major delay in a particular decision during the war derided by the West was attributed to completing plans "by the book." He had the firepower to run for a third consecutive term as president by changing the rules, but did not [9] (although he certainly maintained control.)

- Here is a contentious assertion: in his early days as a bureaucrat it was said that he "cannot be bribed." [10] Now he is portrayed as fabulously wealthy, but I have been unable to confirm what seems to be innuendo. Those around him, however, have benefitted enormously from their proximity to power. His top-down control of industry benefitted many close to him, but that could be a consequence of his centralized control of the economy. One can only *infer* that he is profiting.

- His actions in Ukraine could be construed as either an energy grab or defensive tactics to prevent an energy grab.[11] Regardless, the politics are very thick.
- His battles with the oligarchs draw negative press. When asked about it, he simply noted, "They robbed Russia blind." That turns out to be true; none of the oligarchs made their billions fair and square.[12] Although Khodorkovsky spent a decade in Siberia, the location of his confiscated assets remains unclear to me.

I may be forced to back away from some of these points. I blame the utterly worthless Western press for setting me adrift, rudderless on the internet, in my quest for wisdom. Here are thoughts about the war and NATO, from Putin or through his spokesmen in their own words (which, admittedly, are Putin's too). They are revealing.

> Your people do not yet feel an impending sense of danger. That worries me. Can't you see the world is being pulled in an irreversible direction? Meanwhile, people pretend that nothing is going on. I don't know how to get through to you any more.[13]
>
> — Vladimir Putin

> The dollar enjoyed great trust around the world. But for some reason it is being used as a political weapon, imposing restrictions ... the U.S. dollar will collapse soon.
>
> — Vladimir Putin, 2021

Imposing sanctions is the logical continuation and the distillation of the irresponsible and short-sighted policy of the U.S. and EU countries' governments and central banks ... The global economy and global trade as a whole have suffered a major blow, as did trust in the U.S. dollar as the main reserve currency. The illegitimate freezing of some of the currency reserves of the Bank of Russia marks the end of the reliability of so-called first-class assets ... Now everybody knows that financial reserves can simply be stolen.[14]

— Vladimir Putin

When the territorial integrity of our country is threatened, we, of course, will use all the means at our disposal to protect Russia and our people. This is not a bluff. And those who try to blackmail us with nuclear weapons should know that the weathervane can turn and point towards them.[15]

— Vladimir Putin

During the time of the Soviet Union the role of the state in the economy was made absolute, which eventually led to the total noncompetitiveness of the economy ... I am sure no one would want history to repeat itself.

— Vladimir Putin, communist, 2012

It is extremely alarming that elements of the U.S. global defense system are being deployed near Russia. The Mk 41 launchers, which are located in Romania and are to be deployed in Poland, are adapted for launching the Tomahawk strike missiles. If this infrastructure continues to move forward, and if U.S. and NATO missile systems are deployed in Ukraine, their flight time to Moscow will be only 7–10 minutes, or even five minutes for hypersonic systems. This is a huge challenge for us, for our security.[16]

— Vladimir Putin, December 21, 2021

The Russian President made clear that President Biden's proposals did not really address the central, key elements of Russia's initiatives either with regards to non-expansion of NATO, or non-deployment of strike weapons systems on Ukrainian territory ... To these items, we have received no meaningful response.[17]

— Yuri Ushakov, a top foreign policy adviser to Putin, February 12, 2022

Do you know that 450 individuals were arrested after entering the Congress? They came there with political demands.

— Vladimir Putin, 2021

We are not threatening anyone ... We have made it clear that any further NATO movement to the east is unacceptable. There's nothing unclear about this. We aren't deploying our missiles to the border of the United States, but the United States *is* deploying their missiles to the porch of our house. Are we asking too much? We're just asking that they not deploy their attack systems to our home ... What is so hard to understand about that? [18]

— Vladimir Putin

Our mistake was we trusted you too much, and your mistake was you took advantage of that.[19]

— Vladimir Putin to the U.S. on NATO incursion, 2017

No matter how much Western and so-called supranational elites strive to preserve the existing order of things, a new era is coming, a new stage in world history. And only truly sovereign states can ensure high dynamics for growth and become an example for others.[20]

— Vladimir Putin

We do not care about the eyes of the West. I don't think there's even room for maneuver left any more. Because both [Prime Minister Boris] Johnson and [Foreign Secretary Liz] Truss say publicly: "We must defeat Russia, we must bring Russia to its knees." Go on, then, do it.[21]

— Sergey Lavrov, Foreign Minister of Russia

You can't feed anyone with paper—you need food; and you can't heat anyone's home with these inflated capitalizations—you need energy. The United States is practically pushing Europe toward deindustrialization in a bid to get its hands on the entire European market. These European elites understand everything—they do, but they serve the interests of others.[22]

— Vladimir Putin

We are actively engaged in reorienting our trade flows and foreign economic contacts towards reliable international partners, primarily the BRICS countries.[23]

— Vladimir Putin

If the West continues to pump Ukraine full of weaponry out of impotent rage or a desire to exacerbate the situation ... then that means our geographical tasks will move even further from the current line.[24]

— Sergey Lavrov

The game of nominal value of money is over, as this system does not allow us to control the supply of resources ... Our product, our rules. We don't play by the rules we didn't create.[25]

— Alexei Miller, CEO of Gazprom

> Any fourth-grade history student knows socialism
> has failed in every country, at every time in history.
>
> — Vladimir Putin, 2014 (disputed)

Does that sound like the rantings of an unstable personality? Putin's comments also foreshadow what the brawl is about.

> War is not only a military opposition on Ukrainian
> land. It is also a fierce battle in the informational
> space.
>
> — Zelensky, fighting WW III on Twitter

Volodymyr Zelensky rose to become the elected leader of Ukraine in 2019. He is a colorful character married to a hot wife, consistent with his role as a trained media star, with a law degree to boot. One is struck by similarities between Volo's TV presence and the SNL "sprockets skit."

A highly successful 2019 presidential run rode the back of promises to clean up the corruption in Ukraine, said to be one of the most corrupt countries in the world.[26] Volo's ties with the WEF and Klaus Schwab don't instill confidence.[27] By Ukrainian standards he is a legitimately wealthy man, but his actual net worth is unclear. He has holdings in several companies with ties to Ukrainian Nazis (see below),[28] real estate in several countries,[29,30] ties to Russian oligarchs,[31,32] the backing of a sketchy Ukrainian billionaire,[33,34,35,36,37] and a series of offshore accounts awkwardly leaked in the Pandora Papers.[38,39]

Given the levels of corruption in Ukraine, none of this is very surprising. Rumors of him being a billionaire oligarch have been actively fact-checked,[40] but his oligarchical status seems sound. I have no trouble imagining that Volo was not a billionaire in 2021 but became one in 2022, given the massive and untraced dollar flows into Ukraine. Every time Vlad and Volo seemed to be getting along, more NATO money showed up.

Rep. Paul Gosar, DDS ✓   ...
@RepGosar

Zelensky made $100 million last year as a public servant somehow. Where do you think a sizeable chunk of that $40 billion is really going? We shouldn't be sending a dime, especially not until our long list of problems at home are solved.

3:02 PM · May 11, 2022 · Twitter for Android

9,035 Retweets   **631** Quote Tweets   **40.8K** Likes

Where Politicians Are Named in the Pandora Papers

Countries with the most politicians included in the Pandora Papers release

Ukraine	38
Russia	19
United Arab Emirates	11
Honduras	11
Colombia	11
Nigeria	10
UK	9
Brazil	9
Angola	9

Source: ICIJ

statista

Despite his Jewish roots, Zelensky is affiliated with the ruthless and decidedly antisemitic Azov Battalion. My mental construct is that the Azov Battalion is akin to the Mexican drug cartels—what it lacks in numbers, it makes up for with ruthlessness. His gazillionaire patron is said to be funding the Azov boys,[41] but with the big money coming in from NATO/CIA sources.[42,43]

Ritter posited that the Azovs promised Volo a horrible death if he didn't cooperate.[44,45] Ritter also suggested that early in the conflict the Rooskies felt they could work with Volo, and positioned an extraction team nearby in case he needed help. Strange world.

> We're supposed to just veer away from the narrative that was being pushed just a couple of years ago. What the f*ck is that? What is that?[46]
>
> — Joe Rogan, about pre-war "Zelensky the Nazi"

Volo was absolutely the perfect guy to win the hearts, minds, and wallets of the world, tapping into a combination of charm, fluent English, and theatrical skills. Did I already mention the hot wife? It was a brilliant campaign, aided by the U.S. tech giants and their propaganda machines,[47] Hollywood stars and global elite,[48,49,50] all visiting Kyiv with remarkable ease, given it's a putative war zone.

Volo was even hitting up Xi Jinping to help rebuild Ukraine,[51] despite China's perceived relationship with Russia. I'm surprised he didn't start a SPAC and sell NFTs. *Time* magazine had him as a frontrunner on its list of "favorites to win the Nobel Peace Prize," which is funny when juxtaposed against his contemporaneous call for a full-blown war to be initiated by an alliance of 30 countries against a nuclear superpower.[52,53]

We therefore humbly call upon you, the Committee, to consider: Extending and thereby re-opening the nomination procedure for the Nobel Peace Prize until March 31, 2022 to allow for a Nobel Peace Prize nomination for President Zelensky and the people of Ukraine.[54]

— Letter from 36 current and former European politicians

He got *Time's* participation trophy.

The U.S. has been pouring money and weapons into Ukraine throughout the war. I spitball it at $100 billion.[55,56]

The Ukrainian lobby in Canada, with backing from Chrystia Freeland, dropped a billion dollars under Operation UNIFIER[57] to train Ukrainian neo-Nazis. In denying it, Canadian authorities admitted the Azov guys were not good people.

Irish taxpayers are giving money for "Ukraine's current and future needs" even though they have no ties to NATO.[58] The UK committed to provide 6,000 missiles and to pay Ukrainian soldiers and pilots.[59]

Biden slipped up[60] and said we had boots on the ground, contrary to his pledge.[61,62] Did anybody doubt this? Those sophisticated weapons aren't gonna ~~shoot~~ inspect themselves. Recall that we had advisors in Vietnam in 1962. How did *that* work out?

Two "advisors" were grabbed by the Rooskies. Their whereabouts are unknown to me.[63]

It's not clear whether Volo simply overplayed his hand or something politically deeper occurred, but questions of waste and mismanagement of resources began to surface.[64,65,66,67] While mooching billions, which showed up suspiciously before the bars opened every Friday night, he was threatening to default on Ukrainian debt.[68] The cash was said to "dissolve into a black hole of secrecy, corruption, deceit, and now, default." [69] The weapons disappeared into the black market.[70]

And then there is the FTX-DNC connection that I described in Part One. CBS News buried a documentary on graft associated with the military support for Ukraine because Volo's supporters and the military–industrial complex were not happy.[71,72] Protests around Europe suggested that Johannes Sixpack was growing weary of their sacrifice for a proxy war.[73]

> Show a little more gratitude.[74]
>
> — Joe Biden, to Zelensky

Volo showed his dark side in the pre-war era when his regime banned the teaching of kids in Russian in the ethnically Russian-rich eastern provinces.[75] A 2019 video shows him ranting about how his army is ready to go to war in the Donbas.[76] I have no idea if pre-war atrocities (below) committed by the Azov punks can be hung on the Zelensky regime, but the U.S. buck stops at the top.

> For the truth about the Zelensky regime, Google these names: Voldymyr Struk Denis Kireev Mikhail & Aleksander Kononovich Nestor Shufrych Yan Taksyur Dmitri Djangirov Elena Berezhnaya Once again: If you haven't heard from me in 12 hours or more, put my name on this list.
>
> — Gonzalo Lira, journalist of unknown credibility

While Volo was charming the world out of tens of billions of dollars, he was also doing things you might expect from the president of a profoundly corrupt and authoritarian state.

- He unplugged three television networks that included the voices of his political opponents, even though they had shown no support for Russia.[77]
- He banned and seized the assets of OPPL, Ukraine's second-largest political party and his direct opposition. They were prohibited from "all activity within Ukraine." [78] He included ten other smaller parties in the purge.[79]

- He imprisoned local political opponents [80] and tried to extradite and imprison others abroad, despite there being no evidence they were supporting Russia.
- The dismissal of senior officials raised more than a few bushy eyebrows. [81,82]
- He banned Christianity—the Ukrainian Orthodox Church—as of December 2022, and seized its property. [83]
- Ukrainian authorities threatened all-expense-paid stays in the gulags for 18–60-year-olds who used to stay and fight for the homeland. [84] Some are being shot, although this may be unofficial action by the Azov Boys. [85]

Tucker Carlson took the homogenous Western narrative to task for claiming that Ukraine is a democracy, [86] and *all* Bible-thumping politicians on the right and sanctimonious politicians on the left for their silence. I know why many hate him—I did too—but he is one of the few conservative talking heads who crosses the center line and touches third rails. He is the mirror image of Bill Maher.

> The U.S. is the most warlike country on earth.
>
> — Jimmy Carter

One of Volo's most inexplicable moves was to put out a hitlist—whether metaphorical or real is unknowable—of Westerners seemingly not buying his story. [87,88,89] The list features such luminaries as Marine Le Pen, Tulsi Gabbard, Glenn Greenwald, Jeff Sachs, Scott Ritter, and Rand Paul. [90] Seems he overplayed *that* hand.

He also called for prosecution of U.S. and European megabank CEOs for "committing war crimes" because of their

Russian ties,[91] after reaching out directly to them, to no avail. Dude: you cannot manhandle bankers like Canadian truckers.

> After the fall of the Soviet Union, there was a near universal understanding among political leaders that NATO expansion would be a foolish provocation against Russia. How naive we were to think the military–industrial complex would allow such sanity to prevail.
>
> — Chris Hedges, *very* left-wing independent journalist

NATO (the North Atlantic Treaty Organization) was formed in 1949 as a post-WW II association of nations whose primary purpose was to oppose the rising power of the Soviet Union. By design, it explicitly posed an existential risk to the Soviets, but that is not to say that NATO always behaved aggressively.

After a lifetime of immersion in the Cold War, I had two thoughts when the Soviet Union collapsed: (a) "Holy shit!" and (b) a few years later, "Who is going to oppose us?" Pulling away one of two equal and opposite forces produces a huge power shift.

I remember reading of Jeff Sachs' assurances to the former Soviets that there would be a Marshall Plan-like response from the West. It never materialized, because without the Soviet threat, who needs a Marshall Plan?

Amidst the uncertainty of the Soviet Union splintering into a collection of directionless Warsaw Pact nations and the nervousness of a reuniting Germany, NATO promised Russia that if Russia didn't push to reassemble the Warsaw Pact nations, NATO would not push eastward to absorb them. Declassified documents from U.S. and Russian archives [92,93] revealed that Yeltsin was assured the "Partnership for Peace" was not a NATO expansion, and Russia would be included.

Well, as the agreement with Yeltsin was being worked out, NATO's expansion was already secretly underway. Secretary of State Warren Christopher later said that the drunken Yeltsin had vodka goggles on and didn't realize that the West planned to "lead to gradual expansion of NATO." [94] The written record backs Yeltsin. Bill Clinton started the move in 1997. [95]

> Explicitly calling Putin a war criminal and for his removal from power meaningfully increases the risk of either chemical or nuclear weapons being used in Ukraine. [96]
>
> — Niall Ferguson, Harvard University and the Hoover Institute

One of the legends of the Cold War, George Kennan, called the expansion "the most fateful error of American policy in the entire post-Cold War era." [97] The late Russian expert, Stephen Cohen, was hypercritical of the demonization of Russia (Russophobia). [98]

A younger Joe Biden admitted that bringing Baltic states into NATO would be a mistake. [99] As the tweeter disrespectfully noted, "Even shit for brains knew." Some time later, Vice President Shit-for-Brains was heard cat-calling Russia for its concerns over NATO's expansion. [100]

Ukraine is strategically critical for Russia, but I cannot find evidence that Russia wants possession of Ukraine. There is, however, copious evidence that Russia perceives NATO's control over Ukraine a profound threat. NATO's relentless sanctions and threats against Russia over decades leaves little doubt that the Russian view is sound. [101] The U.S. could and would sever Russia's ties to Ukraine in a heartbeat. Within the halls of power, the Cold War never ended.

> The decision for the U.S. and its allies to expand NATO into the east was decisively made in 1993. I called this a big mistake from the very beginning. It was definitely a violation of the spirit of the statements and assurances made to us in 1990.[102]
>
> — Mikhail Gorbachev, former leader of the Soviet Union

> The bottom line is that the strategic interests of the United States are to prevent Russia from becoming a hegemon. And the strategic interests of Russia are not to allow the U.S. close to its borders.[103]
>
> — George Friedman, founder of Stratfor, 2014

NATO and the CIA have been dumping money and weapons into Ukraine for years.[104,105] CIA operatives have been crawling all over Ukraine, arming and training troops for a potential conflict with Russia. This is provocative, but those actions are neither legally nor tactically the same as Ukraine being *in* NATO.

The Maidan coup in 2014,[106,107] sponsored by the CIA and Ukrainian oligarchs, brought U.S. puppet Arseniy Yatsenyuk and his Nazi loyalists to power.[108,109] (Funny trivia point: Ihor Kolomoyskyi, the oligarch who funded the coup, owns Burisma Holdings.) George Friedman, the head of Stratfor, a private intelligence firm, called it "the most blatant coup in history."[110] That's a high bar. It also led to some hilarity as super-neocon and Dick Cheney protegée, Victoria

Nuland,[111,112] was recorded planning the swap and saying, "Fuck the EU." She now works for Biden, or vice versa.

> The extent of the Obama administration's meddling in Ukraine's politics was breathtaking ... One can legitimately condemn some aspects of Moscow's behavior, but the force of America's moral outrage is vitiated by the stench of U.S. hypocrisy.[113]
>
> — Ted Galen Carpenter in *Foreign Affairs*, 2017

There was a phase change in 2014. Mearsheimer says that was when NATO began training thousands of Ukrainian troops per year and providing more money and weapons, eventually with the help of Erik Prince of Blackwater fame.[114] Joint military exercises were designed to facilitate "interoperability" so that they could work with NATO forces.

Here are Senators Graham, McCain, and Klobuchar rallying the Ukrainian troops in 2016.[115] "Klobuchar" is a Ukrainian word and loosely translates as "insufferable, self-serving neocon."

By 2021, NATO-trained troops were holding war exercises on Russia's borders.[116] Meanwhile, between 2014 and 2022, the civil war in the Donbas killed an estimated 14,000 people as Ukrainian Nationalists put some whoop-asskyy on ethnic-Russian separatists.[117]

The **Azov Battalion** has deep roots. For a crash course on its origins, the documentary "Ukraine on Fire" (2016) is probably a good place to start.[118] An off-off-Broadway analyst named The Last American Vagabond conducted an interesting, well-documented, and extemporaneous analysis, pulling together connections of fascist groups around the globe under the umbrella called the Azov Movement, all using remarkably common logos and symbolism.[119,120] This Twitter thread gives some backdrop.[121]

The Ukrainian Nazis—called "nationalists" by news sanitizers—trace back to at least WW II. Ukraine was split into two factions. The "nationalists" led by Stepan Bandera in western Ukraine fought with the Germans against the Soviets. They were brutal ethnic cleansers and antisemites.[122] To this day, the so-called Banderites celebrate Bandera's birthday.[123]

During the Cold War the U.S. cozied up to him, as delineated in a great book, *The Devil's Chessboard*, [124] with the CIA providing cover for numerous atrocities.

Bandera was whacked in 1959 by either the Soviets or the CIA.

While the Nazi presence in Ukraine is thoroughly documented, what may surprise some is their postwar fascist influence throughout Europe. A documentary recounting the profound role played by closet fascists in founding the EU is both convincing and disturbing.[125]

ADL

ADL ☑
@ADL · Follow
⊘ Official

This Ukrainian extremist group, called The Azov Battalion, has ties to neo-Nazis and white supremacists. Our latest report on international white supremacy details how they try to connect with like-minded extremists from the US: adl.org/resources/repo...

The ADL issues statement declaring Ukraine's Azov Battalion no longer 'far-right'

 ALEXANDER RUBINSTEIN · DECEMBER 8, 2022

Prior to 2022, the existence of a dangerous Nazi population in Western Ukraine was widely covered and uncontested. Since the onset of the war, the press has tried to erase that history. Recall Nina Jankowicz's role (see Part One).[126] I suspect that earlier efforts to de-Nazify the public record would have been more aggressive, had NATO analysts believed that Putin would make his move.

Western Media before Feb. 2022:

In the late 1980s the Banderites rejuvenated a neo-Nazi movement and, with NATO assistance, incited civil unrest prior to the U.S.-led 2014 coup.[127] The Banderites were also in cahoots with the cops during brutal and well-funded "Maydan" protests. Victoria Nuland *et al.* realized the Nazis were their best shot at giving Russia guff.[128] There are also the usual stories of George Soros being involved. Contacts with McCain, Graham, and Biden attest to the level of U.S. involvement.

The coup eventually ousted highly flawed Putin puppet Prime Minister Viktor Yanukovych and replaced him with highly flawed U.S. puppet Prime Minister Arseniy Yatsenyuk.

> It was one of the most provoked invasions of our lifetimes because of the West dumping its arms in Ukraine.
>
> — Max Blumenthal, independent journalist

Following Ukraine's 2014 coup, the Banderites consolidated the Azov Battalion while embarking on a campaign of terror against ethnic Russians in the Donbas, all coordinated by CIA director John Brennan.[129] Videos show them burning the trade union headquarters, killing 41 people trapped inside[130] while the police stood by. Obama praised these freedom fighters for showing "remarkable restraint." [131]

The Azovs set up headquarters in Mariupol, which, not coincidentally, was a primary Russian military target during the war.

For a real crash course on these guys, search "Azov Battalion" on Google or Twitter, setting a custom date range before January 2022.[132,133] Older BBC and *Time* documentaries show Nazis behaving badly.[134,135] The evidence of Azov brutality is unassailable.[136,137] Getting a reliable head count of Azovs, however, is like counting soldiers in a drug cartel (not easy).

> I will not call people in Donbas Ukrainians; we don't need them. When Ukrainian tanks enter Donetsk, they (local residents) will be destroyed.[138]
>
> — Ukrainian soldier who identifies as a Nazi

Attempts to rehabilitate the Banderite and Azov image include renaming streets across Ukraine after Banderite heroes.[139] The *Times of Israel* was not happy.

The CIA's interest in exploiting the Banderites and Azov Battalion, and the absence of image rehabilitation until the war began, may attest to the CIA miscalculating Putin's willingness to fight. Given recent efforts to root out Nazis and white supremacists from the U.S. military—no doubt a propaganda lie for some other purpose—it's ironic that the U.S. and Ukraine were the only votes against a UN resolution condemning the Ukrainian neo-Nazis.[140]

Zelensky was also having trouble hiding Azov shenanigans. Western journalists from the Associated Press accompanied Zelensky's troops as they kidnapped Ukrainians who questioned the regime.[141] This was for show, but some wondered what happens when the cameras are turned off.[142]

Videos of the Azov thugs beating civilians and torturing Russian captives are legion,[143,144,145,146] being taken down quickly but propagating like Tribbles.[147] One shows a Ukrainian field doctor saying that they are treating Russian captives who have been castrated. Another shows the Azovs doing the nasty.[148,149]

In short, it is very difficult to find redeeming traits in the Azov Battalion.

Ukraine violated the Minsk deal, Zelenskiy tripled attacks on Donbas and pushed Putin to a special operation that was supposed to last a week but escalated after the West sent money and weapons to Kyiv.[150]

— Silvio Berlusconi, former prime minister of Ital

WHAT PROMPTED THE INVASION?

A Rand Corporation white paper described how we would arrive at war with Russia.[1,2] Think tanks aren't paid by the Pentagon to study issues but rather to propagandize them.[3] Rand summarized ways to trigger incidents between Russia and NATO.

> From the Russian leadership's perspective, the theater itself could not be of greater significance; Ukraine has long been seen as a core national security concern ... This Perspective summarizes the most-plausible pathways that could lead to a Russian decision to target NATO member states during the current conflict, describes the conditions under which Moscow might undertake such actions, and lays out how U.S. and NATO actions— including ongoing military assistance to Ukraine— could affect each pathway's likelihood.
>
> — Rand Corporation, July 2022

Cui bono? Well, for starters, the military–industrial complex benefits from the billions of dollars. Lloyd Austin was on Raytheon's board of directors before the revolving door led him to become Secretary of Defense.[4] Former CIA director Gina Haspel went in the other direction, joining the board of BAE Systems as BAE became the chief supplier of artillery to Ukraine.[5] It is nice to see Gina land on her feet.

These guys are making a killing by killing. There will *never* be a promised "peace dividend."

> Everything that's being shipped into Ukraine today, of course, is coming out of stockpiles, either at DOD or from our NATO allies, and that's all great news. Eventually, we'll have to replenish it, and we will see a benefit to the business.[6]

— Greg Hayes, CEO of Raytheon

> The barking of NATO at the gates of Russia ... weapons are being tested in that land ... Wars are fought for this: to test the weapons we have produced ... The arms trade is a scandal; few oppose it.[7]

— The Pope, on what prompted Putin's incursion

One could ask why Russia waited so long. If all hell was breaking out in eastern Ukraine, why care *now?* The obvious answer is that the seriousness of the move would give any leader pause, but there were events transpiring that prompted Russia to act.

Jacques Baud says that the shelling of the Donbas on February 16 made it clear to Putin that a big move against the ethnic Russians had started.[8] Some suggest those same events alerted the Biden administration that shit was about to get real, although it is impossible to believe the U.S. didn't instigate the escalation.

> Ukraine should renounce its NATO aspirations and declare neutrality as part of a wider European security deal between the West and Russia.[9]

Zelensky is said to have overtly sandbagged any negotiations. While most military powers negotiate first and then go to war, the Russians fight and negotiate concurrently. Destroying Kyiv or Zelensky was not in their plans because it would leave no negotiators. Russia's objective was to de-Nazify and demilitarize Ukraine, not beat them, nor destroy infrastructure that would have to be rebuilt. That is also why the fighting in Kharkiv and Mariupol—the home of the Azov Battalion—became particularly intense.[10]

The Biden administration is so intent on punishing Putin, it can hardly focus on the Ukrainians who are dying every day.[11]

— Defense Intelligence Agency (DIA) officer

In November 2021, Antony Blinken reaffirmed Ukraine's right to join NATO and listed Russia's indiscretions, including its "continuing malign behavior."[12]

In December the Russians warned us they were "about to lose their shit" and proposed a treaty,[13] asking for NATO's assurance they would not further weaponize Ukraine. We told them: "Bite me."[14] We did not merely disagree; we blew them off. This is Mearsheimer's key point: we are no longer credible negotiators.

On February 21 and 24 Putin delivered speeches setting out Russia's gripes and its need to "demilitarize" and "de-Nazify" Ukraine. Steve Walt says Putin was acting rationally, given that NATO's next move was unclear. The Russians had no reason to take our stated intentions on good faith. The previous promises to exclude Ukraine from joining NATO were by handshake—according to Mearsheimer, a common protocol in diplomatic circles—but Putin wanted it in writing this time (as he lamented in his interviews with Oliver Stone.) A written promise could be broken, but it would be harder to break.

> Putin tried desperately to get the British, the French, the Germans, and us to understand that his Russian citizens should be treated equally before the law just like Ukrainian citizens inside this large multi-ethnic state. (But) Zelensky and his friends said "No. Either you become what we are or you get out." [15]
>
> — Colonel Douglas Macgregor

Some think the war was triggered not by the threat of a NATO incursion *per se* but when Ukrainian troops started markedly ramping up shelling of ethnic Russian Ukrainians in the Donbas.[16] Nine days later, Putin made the move with a "special military operation."

Some analysts with nuanced views believe NATO could have stopped the war in those last few days, but NATO had no intention of diffusing the conflict.[17] It appears that Putin accelerated the attack by several days due to intelligence suggesting imminent mass atrocities in eastern Ukraine.[18]

> Use up the Irish. Their dead cost nothing.
>
> — King Edward I (Edward Longshanks), *Braveheart*

Jumping ahead a little, during the war NATO fanned the flames by calling for the accelerated inclusion of Finland and Sweden.[19] One neocon was ranting that the Kremlin didn't give a shit, arguing that Russia's obsession over Ukraine was hypocrisy. What this NATO pimp failed to grasp was that he was making the case for Ukraine being a special issue to Russia. Also, the Kremlin *did* object strenuously to NATO's overtures to Finland and Sweden, and *had* previously expressed grave concerns if Sweden and Finland started to be weaponized.[20]

Some suggest that the move toward Sweden and Finland is evidence that Ukraine is soon to be under Russian control, and that NATO is repositioning for the next brawl.[21]

Murad Gazdiev ✔
@MuradGazdiev

The Russian Foreign Ministry has called on Western media outlets to publish a full list of dates on which Russia will invade Ukraine for the year ahead, so Russian diplomats can schedule their vacations accordingly.

This is not satire. They did this

3:20 AM · Feb 16, 2022 · Twitter for iPhone

3,193 Retweets   **572** Quote Tweets   **10.1K** Likes

THE DRUMS OF WAR

The war began paradoxically. In breathless press conferences Jake Sullivan claimed the attack was coming, but the reporters simply did not believe him, as no evidence was provided. British defense secretary Ben Wallace said it was "highly likely" that Russia *will* attack Ukraine.[1,2] By contrast, the Chinese Foreign Ministry said that "the U.S. has been fanning the threat of war, artificially creating a tense atmosphere, which has dealt a serious blow to the economy, social stability and living conditions of the people of Ukraine."[3] The Chinese, of course, would never lie.

However, even Ukraine's Defense Minister noted, "Our intelligence sees every move that could pose a potential threat to Ukraine. We estimate the probability of a large-scale escalation as low."[4,5] David Arakhamia of Kyiv's parliament said he was "99.9% confident that nothing will happen."[6,7] Zelensky claimed that the U.S. was "provoking panic" and demanded to see firm proof.[8,9]

A Russian spokesperson requested facetiously, "I'd like to request US and British disinformation—Bloomberg, the *New York Times* and *The Sun* media outlets—to publish the schedule for our upcoming invasions for the year."[10]

Zelensky then suggested the war would start February 16, but that was later claimed to be sarcasm emerging from his comedic roots.[11] He's a hoot.

This veneer of chaos and confusion, however, is consistent with the general idea that the U.S.—oops, I meant NATO—was itching to spark a proxy war that nobody else was thrilled about. A German accused the U.S. of wreaking havoc deliberately to disrupt Russian attack plans.[12]

My spidey sense was piqued by two independent emails sent to me from unrecognized sources, noting that (a) there was already shelling in the Donbas region of Ukraine *by Ukrainians*, and (b) large Ukrainian forces had been amassing for months. This was common knowledge, but I knew *nothing* about the civil war until then.

> Putin is not intentionally attacking civilians ... he is mindful that he needs to limit damage in order to leave an out for negotiations.[13]
>
> — William M. Arkin, *Newsweek*, March 22

The Russian state department eventually sent a flight to Washington, D.C. to pick up its "Russian intelligence agents" from the embassy,[14] and the war started, but at a crawl. I drove my wife nuts every night, declaring, "This doesn't look like a war to me." If you wanna see serious war footage, check out Baghdad on Day One [15] of the Iraq War or even watch *Saving Private Ryan* for the ninth time.

The media covered human interest stories about how awful it was, showed photos of burned-out cars and the occasional explosion in the middle of some street or vacant lot that looked like a stick of dynamite (or M-80) being detonated rather safely.[16] The larger explosions seemed to miss their targets,[17] and huge explosions were so far away that there was no indication of what blew up.

> I know it's hard ... to swallow that the carnage and destruction could be much worse than it is, but that's what the facts show.[18]
>
> — DIA analyst

It's odd that the windows survived a car-flipping blast (top), while it appears that a MOAB turned a goat grazing in a vacant field into pink mist. Early footage from Mariupol looked more like grinding poverty from decades-long destruction and decay than a fresh war zone.[19,20] Nightly news footage was highly repetitive, showing the same buildings from different angles. Was that all the media could find? On-the-ground interviews were either content-free or featured people who seemed unaware what was happening while expressing mixed emotions about Putin versus Zelensky.[21] A British journalist went looking for the war and found shelling of Ukrainians by Ukrainians.[22] Another found neither a war nor other journalists.[23]

You ask, "Well, what about these horrors, you idiot?"

Well, those are horrific scenes, but they are (a) Detroit; (b) Ukraine, 2022; (c) Baltimore; (d) Donbas, 2014; (e) the South Bronx; (f) Mariupol, 2016; (g) Yemen, and; (h) Minneapolis, 2020. See how easy it would be for the media to dupe you?

I was not alone in my doubts. A powerful analysis by William Arkin of *Newsweek* made a strong case that Putin was pulling his punches in order to avoid infrastructure destruction and civilian casualties.

> Heartbreaking images make it easy for the news to focus on the war's damage to buildings and lives. But in proportion to the intensity of the fighting (or Russia's capacity), things could indeed be much worse.[24]

Scott Ritter, the U.S. marine who drew scorn from Joe Biden for saying Iraq did not have weapons of mass destruction,[25] *predicted* Russia's WW I-like invasion strategy. In particular, he said that with Russia's small invasion force, it did not intend to occupy territory. Ritter also predicted that Putin would draw Ukrainian troops into the cities, to defend them. Once accomplished, he would avoid urban warfare, circling the cities.

You may recall the Western press slobbering over Putin's retreats as evidence Russia was getting toe-tagged. Colonel Macgregor concurred with Ritter that calling Russian moves "retreats" was silly.[26] Both Macgregor and CIA analyst Jacques Baud noted that Ukraine was fighting for territory while Russia was fighting to demilitarize and de-Nazify Ukraine, with an interest only in *tactically important* territory.[27] Retired Colonel David Johnson of the Rand Corporation and the Modern War Institute at West Point insinuated that the Western press was looking through beer goggles.[28] Battles in the Donbas were said by blogger Will Schryver to be akin to the Maginot Line, with the Rooskies dealing with long-prepared fixed fortifications so efficiently that the strategy "will be studied in war colleges" for years to come.[29]

Before moving on to specific events, here are some random observations from early in the conflict that caught my eye as odd or unexpected.

- In May a Russian soldier was convicted of a war crime for shooting a 62-year-old civilian.[30] This is an oddly small crime for war.
- Despite headlines and breathless narratives, in the early days of the war it proved exceedingly difficult to discern which battles were being won, and by whom. Videos showed blurred-out street signs.[31] Putative Russian tanks lacked the traditional markings. It was the fog of war.
- A Reuters story describing how Ukrainian troops repelled a Russian incursion in the Sumy region showed a picture of guys with paintball guns.[32,33] Apparently, "Big Paintball," also known as the "paintball–industrial complex," is getting its cut. Recall that ABC showed a hellacious fight against Syrians ... filmed at a military gun range in the Midwest.[34] Americans got duped by those images too.

> Long-range artillery is very, very important. But so is the hand-to-hand insurgency that we are hoping to see in eastern Ukraine, in the territory that's already been occupied by the Russians.[35]
>
> — Senator Richard Blumenthal, armchair quarterback. Is he volunteering?

- Three weeks into the war, the United Nations reported 596 deaths, including 43 children. Biden's drone strike in Afghanistan killed six kids in a microsecond. I suspect the Iraq War killed more than 596 people in its first few seconds.
- A pregnant woman in Ukraine scrambling from the horrors of war turned out to be a prominent Instagram model Wagging the Dog.[36]
- Two British mercenaries (MI6, maybe?) were arrested by the Rooskies and taken to court for trying to kill Rooskies.[37,38] Seems like a logical charge to me. A couple of Americans got picked up too.[39]
- Ukrainians standing next to a long-defunct factory refused to evacuate because they were "waiting for the Russians to arrive and put the factory back into production." [40] The plan is that "they will soon be repairing Russian tanks, and then they will have bread on the table again." They also griped that only the wealthy and those ideologically supportive of the Kyiv regime could evacuate.
- A putative Russian attack on the holocaust museum did not hold up to scrutiny by the Israeli press.[41]
- Russian attacks on a nuclear plant made no sense, given that the Russians controlled it, and that UN inspectors invited in by the Russians found no problems either.[42] Anyone can hit the "broadside of a cooling tower."

> The media does not allow any word against Ukrainian actions. I've asked around to friends and they say, "Yeah, Jeff. Of course it's Ukraine shelling the power plant." [43]
>
> — Jeff Sachs

- "Heroic Ukrainian freedom fighters" on Snake Island who flipped off the Russian navy and were said to be "martyred" by the Rooskies are doing fine after all.[44]

- Claims of mass rape of Ukrainians by Russian soldiers played well on Western news outlets [45] but did not age well when Westerners checked the story, eventually leading to the firing of the Ukrainian official offering up these fibs.[46] The propaganda defeat [47] was simply ignored by some human rights groups looking for clicks.[48]

- Putative mercenaries were occasionally identified, but whether they were ex-military Westerners with Ukrainian sympathies or state-sanctioned NATO troops is difficult to say.[49,50]

- The Biden administration's accusations of genocide by Russian troops [51] were called bullshit by French President Macron and by our Pentagon and U.S. intelligence officials.[52]

- A German journalist is facing a three-year prison sentence for writing about Ukraine with a Russian slant.[53] Remind me: which country is the totalitarian state?

- Gold teeth attributed to a Roosky torture chamber were traced to a dentist who had collected them over his multi-decade career.[54] The photo also featured a dildo pulled from ... never mind.

- Ukraine's Post Office issued a postage stamp commemorating the bombing of the Kerch Bridge connecting Russia to Crimea *on the day it was bombed.*[55] That stamp may become a valuable collectible. It was also Putin's seventieth birthday.[56] Somebody has a sense of humor.

- While Zelensky and NATO blamed mass graves on torture, reporters noted that the graves were orderly, and that it looked like the victims had died from artillery wounds.[57]

- Western reports that the Rooskies were going to use a dirty bomb—a normal bomb impregnated with radioactive debris—never materialized, and never made sense, because a dirty bomb would offer no tactical gain.

- Images of dead Ukrainians strewn alongside a road in Bucha lit up the international presses. The problem was that the Ukrainians had "liberated" Bucha on March 31 and had it "fully under control," according to the mayor. The bodies, however, did not materialize until three days later. OK, shit happens, but the Ukrainian National Police are tight with the ruthless Azov boys known for killing Ukrainians.[58] A former French special ops guy says it was Ukrainians, not Russians, doing the killing.[59]

- Odesa is a port city on the Black Sea, of critical economic and military importance to both the Ukrainians and the Russians. The day after the Russians signed a grain export deal with Turkey, the port suffered an attack. U.S. officials blamed Russia for destroying a shipping port of great importance to Russia. Zelensky agreed with NATO because he won't bite the hand that feeds him money and weapons.[60] The Russians and Turks countered that it was nuts to accuse Russia of attacking a port critical to their needs.[61] Russia eventually admitted to hitting a "military target ... Harpoon missiles," claimed "nobody died," and assured the world the grain deal was still on.[62,63,64]

Some events need more than a bullet. When a Russian missile landed in a train station and killed over fifty Ukrainians, I was reminded that if you wish to learn, post a tweet with an error or omission in it,[65] and sit back and watch.

This is a piece of the deadly missile that killed dozens in Ukraine: discuss.

8:03 AM · Apr 9, 2022

Within minutes, military guys noted that the above photo is of a two-stage unguided "Tochka" missile, and that I was seeing only the jettisoned stage. I learned that the Tochkas had been decommissioned by the Rooskies more than five years ago, and that only the Ukies were using them now,[66] although that has been contested.[67,68]

Apparently, if you know where both stages landed, it is a trivial matter to calculate the origin of a Tochka by extrapolating backward. Doing so pinpointed this missile's source to the heart of Ukrainian-occupied territory.[69]

The Rooskies came to the same conclusion, but of course that was blocked by Western censors because hearing the other side of any story is counterproductive.[70] The recurring theme is that Ukrainians kill Ukrainians, especially when billions in aid are at stake.

The media told us a gripping story about Ukrainian troops from the Azov Battalion under siege in the Azovstahl steel mill in Mariupol. The Russian siege eventually flushed them out.[71] Of course, Putin's demilitarization and de-Nazification plan made this group (and Mariupol) primary targets.

The civilians were offered a free pass out multiple times and, when they finally got out, were surprised to find the rest of the city going about its business. The civilians were referred to by Amnesty International as "human shields," which was said to be a common practice of the Ukrainian troops.[72,73] There were rumors of Western military officers being captured, too.[74]

I would not underwrite the health or life insurance policies of the Azov captives on that bus to Siberia.

PIPELINES, BRIDGES, AND OTHER INFRA-STRUCTURE

> Russia is the most likely suspect.[1]
>
> —John Brennan, former CIA director and the model of honesty, on the pipeline

> *Jeff Sachs:* The destruction of the Nord Stream pipeline ... I would bet was a U.S. action, perhaps U.S. and Poland.[2]
>
> *Tom Keene, interrupting:* Uh, Jeff, we've got to stop there.

By now, pretty much everybody knows that the Nord Stream 2 natural gas pipeline to Europe, and the Kerch Bridge providing critical access to the Russian satellite of Crimea, were blown up. I *suspect* neither event was as damaging as first thought.[3]

The West's immediate reaction was to blame Russia for blowing up its own infrastructure, which is absurd.[4] Fact-checkers attacked "rumors circulating on online forums popular with American conservatives and followers of QAnon," which is comically stupid.[5,6] Some say the British did it for us, but Navy activities in the area days before the explosion are suspicious.[7,8,9,10] The unfiltered Jeff Sachs noted, "We are seeing the behavior of a highly secretive part of our government. There is no doubt." [11,12]

Whether the strike was carried out by the U.S. or one of its proxies—NATO bitches—is irrelevant. Joe Biden *and* neocon Victoria "Fuck the EU" Nuland made statements months earlier that are hard to walk back.[13]

> If Russia invades ... then there will no longer be a Nord Stream 2. We will bring an end to it.[14]
>
> — Joe Biden

> If Russia invades Ukraine, one way or another, Nord Stream 2 will not move forward.
>
> — Victoria Nuland, neocon

Colonel Macgregor,[15] noting the sophistication and tonnage of explosives required to damage the pipeline, asks rhetorically, "Would the Russians destroy their own pipeline? Forty percent of Russian gross domestic product generates foreign currencies that come into the country to purchase natural gas, oil, and coal ... The notion that they did I think is absurd."

Well, Poland's former Minister of Defense Sikorski seemed sure who did it.

Radek Sikorski MEP ✓
@radeksikorski

Thank you, USA.

4:38 PM · Sep 27, 2022 · Twitter for Android

The reason why the U.S. blew it up seems rather straightforward: "Berlin was drifting away from the alliance," threatening to stop sending equipment to Ukraine, and preparing to cut a deal.[17] The Germans can ponder their next move this winter while they shutter industries and freeze their asses off burning firewood[18] to heat their houses. Seems a shame they just shut down their nuke plants.

I would be pissed off *and* self-loathing. The U.S. should benefit from soaring natural gas prices while Germany complains about U.S. profiteering.[19] With three of the four pipelines delivering Russian natural gas to Europe out of commission, Hungary is now the only EU member state still receiving Russian gas.[20] Blowing up Nord Stream 2 has forced Germany into the position of "vassal state" of the U.S.

The United States considers the most dangerous potential alliance to be between Russia and Germany.

— George Friedman, founder of Stratfor, 2014

BIOWEAPONS LABORATORIES

When the Soviet Union toppled, one of the nightmare scenarios was that its dilapidated bioweapons labs were located in collapsing buildings, secured by rusty padlocks, and staffed by heroin addicts possibly looking to raise cash on the black market. This threat is nicely described in Richard Preston's 2001 nail-biter, *Demon in the Freezer*.[1]

Of course, the West then had thirty years to decommission those labs in Ukraine, and you would not dawdle, despite what CNN says.[2]

Well, it appears there are several dozen U.S.-sponsored bioweapons labs in Ukraine (and 336 worldwide).[3,4,5] Those who expressed concerns about this, such as Tulsi Gabbard, were hammered for such hare-brained "Russian-backed conspiracy theories."[6]

However, the Nunn–Lugar Agreement cleared these labs for use in 2005.[7] The Pentagon 'fessed up to there being 46 Ukrainian biolabs,[8,9] and the Rooskies have known about them for years.[10] We were scrambling to get the good stuff back to the U.S.—you know, the deadly shit like modified coronaviruses—before the war started.[11]

Any thought that this is just wild-eyed conspiracy theory was snuffed when Victoria Nuland sheepishly and with cautious word choice admitted they exist.[12]

REPORT

False Claims of U.S. Biowarfare Labs in Ukraine Grip QAnon

The conspiracy theory has been boosted by Russian and Chinese media and diplomats.

By Justin Ling, a journalist based in Toronto.

USA admits there are Biolabs in Ukraine, says if a biological attack happens 'it is Russia's fault'

OpIndia Staff | 9 March, 2022

Uh, Ukraine has, uh, biological research facilities. We are now in fact quite concerned that Russian troops, Russian forces, may be seeking to, uh, gain control of [those labs], so we are working with the Ukrainians on how they can prevent any of those research materials from falling into the hands of Russian forces, should they approach.

— Victoria Nuland, testifying to Congress

SO WE HAD A FEW BIO-LABS IN UKRAINE

Jeff Sachs jumped into the fray again, this time asking the World Health Organization (WHO) to intervene.[13] Seems germane, given that Sachs ran the commission that confirmed that Sars-CoV-2 virus came from such a lab and that the WHO was in full ass-covering mode. Both the Chinese[14] and the Russians[15] drew attention to U.S. bioweapons research leading to the COVID pandemic, including many of the authoritarian implications.[16] The BBC says that healthy newborns in Ukraine have been scooped up and become part of stem cell production facilities. I wonder who sponsored those? [17] All roads really do lead to Ukraine.

> We have approached a fateful moment in world history, not because of global warming, COVID, overpopulation, white racism, or any of the "crises" that an ignorant media hypes, but because we face nuclear war originating in the total stupidity of Western elites.
>
> — P.C. Roberts, former Assistant Secretary of the Treasury

> The great powers have taken over and practically destroyed the UN order over the past several decades. I assume that we're leaving the phase of the special military operation and approaching a major armed conflict, and now the question becomes where is the line, and whether after a certain time—maybe a month or two, even—we will enter a great world conflict not seen since the Second World War.
>
> — Aleksandar Vucic, President of Serbia

NUCLEAR WAR?

In the decades following the Cuban Missile Crisis, no sane person considered nuclear weapons to be tactically viable. All diplomatic channels were designed to avoid Armageddon. Apparently, there are now insane people in positions of power. It is crystal clear that Russian authorities, whether it be Putin, Lavrov, Medvedev, or the Minister of Whatever, are speaking with one voice that to a major degree is Putin's:

> I'm Vladimir Putin, and I approve this message.

NATO's many disparate voices are problematic when it comes to delicate diplomacy. Let's bullet a few (double entendre intended).

- Polish officials claim that the Biden administration is open to letting Poland host U.S. nuclear weapons—"nuclear-sharing."[1] Poland, as you might recall, is on Russia's doorstep.[2,3] Poland's European Parliament Deputy, Radoslaw Sikorski, emerged from his lair yet again, suggesting we give some nukes to Kyiv: "The West has the right to give Ukraine nuclear warheads so that it can protect its independence."[4] My allergic reaction to Sikorski in the Munk debate against Mearsheimer just crystallized. The Russians noted that a nuclear conflict will destroy the European continent.[5]
- Republican Senator Roger Wicker said he wouldn't even rule out a pre-emptive nuclear strike against Russia.[6] Who the fuck asked *you*?
- Secretary of Defense Lloyd Austin's stated goal is to weaken Putin.[7]

> I am here. Standing here. On the northern flank. On the eastern flank. Talking about what we have in terms of the eastern flank in our NATO allies and what is that state at this very moment.[8]
>
> — Kamala Harris in Poland, preventing WW III

- In what may have been the scariest op-ed of the year, uber-neocon John Bolton called for the assassination of Putin: "The whole regime must go." [9]
- Biden said, "For God's sake, this man cannot remain in power." [10] The *Washington Post* called it "the most defiant and aggressive speech about Russia by an American president since Ronald Reagan." Bullshit. Reagan never called for regime change. Also, that was a nice try at equating those two polar opposites.

> Globalists are marching us relentlessly toward this nuclear Armageddon.[11]
>
> — Richard Black, in an open letter to Congress

- Lindsay Graham called for Putin's countrymen to "take him out." [12]
- The Ukrainian military's commander-in-chief suggested, "There is a direct threat of the use, under certain circumstances, of tactical nuclear weapons by the Russian armed forces. It is also impossible to completely rule out the possibility of the direct involvement of the world's leading countries in a 'limited' nuclear conflict." [13,14]

- New York City began playing duck-and-cover anti-nuke ads
  this year.[16] Those were insane sixty years ago.
- The odd part is that the nuclear talks are largely stemming
  from NATO. Many have argued that Russia would not use
  nukes, which are not tactically sound, because they have
  better options.[17] Oddly, Mearsheimer is *not* in that camp.
  He thinks a nuke might be the proximate trigger that brings
  everybody to the negotiating table.

Hats off to French President Emmanuel Macron for
keeping his head while everybody else was losing theirs, by
refusing to describe Russia's actions as genocide: "If Russia had
that objective or was intentionally killing civilians, we'd see a lot
more than less than 0.01 percent in places like Bucha." U.S.
intelligence concurred: "[Genocide] has so far not been
corroborated by information collected by U.S. intelligence
agencies." [18]

WHO IS WINNING?

Quite frankly, I have no idea who is winning this war. With the lack of critical analysis of Russian army movements, the confusion is profound. Undocumented NATO "advisors" doing "onsite weapons inspections" and possibly firing those weapons that are "well beyond the skills of the Ukrainians"[1,2,3] appear to have caused serious damage.

However, Ritter, Macgregor,[4] and ex-CIA analyst Ray McGovern[5] claim that the Russian losses, while more than they expected at the outset, because of the flood of NATO weapons, are grotesquely overstated by Zelensky and the Western press. Macgregor estimated a Russian-to-Ukrainian kill ratio of 5–6:1 in October, and that as of early December, Ukraine had lost an estimated 100,000 troops.[6]

Rumors of Russians running out of tanks went silent as swaths of new tanks appeared.[7] Putin was said to be in huge political trouble or as strong as ever in Russia, depending on who you asked. The claim is that the Rooskies aren't mudders, but once the ground freezes they will play like the Packers on Lambeau Field.

After the bridge and pipeline attacks, Putin ratcheted up the offensive, and the real war appears to have arrived. He appears to be surgically destroying their infrastructure sufficiently to make this winter *very* unpleasant.

> It is of course in the nature of things that, apart from the relative strength of the two armies, a smaller force will be exhausted sooner than a larger one; it cannot run so long a course, and therefore the radius of its theater of operations is bound to be restricted.

The insanity of the statements coming out of the many mouths of NATO leaves me breathless. Putin may have misjudged Ukraine's and Washington's resistance to negotiation. The bellicosity of the self-appointed voices of NATO blowing hot air on the flames means the end of this war is not yet in sight. If you want Putin to say, "Fuck it: let's tear up the joint" in a green-goblin strategy, that is how I would do it.

Sherman took the war to the people by marching on Atlanta. Putin may be following that script now. With negotiation down the drain, the prospects for a peace have become grim and could get worse.

Interviewer: What are the realistic options now available?

John Mearsheimer: There are no options. We're screwed.

HOW DOES IT END?

I could imagine it ending in a whimper, like every big news story that becomes inconvenient. I am sure Kanye, Prince Harry, or Will Smith will provide critical cover. Or somebody will use the N-word.

One of the profound problems, however, is that we do not seem to have concrete plans or motivation to end this war. NATO is comprised of multiple countries. Its human weaponry includes legions of loose cannons loaded with double-digit IQs, all trying to get their fifteen minutes of fame by supporting no-fly zones, sending in U.S. troops, delivering nukes to Ukraine, pre-emptively striking Russia, and whacking Putin.

Even assuming Russia ignores the high noise levels, NATO exists to oppose Russia. Serious spokespersons have openly stated that their objective is to weaken or destroy Putin and Russia. This is an existential risk for Putin and Russia *by definition.* Russia *must* win, and will fight to the death.

Into this politically treacherous plot enters The Squad—the four newly minted Congressional nitwits—and 26 other DNC-spawned representatives with an open letter suggesting the most coherent idea to date: NATO and Russia should get to the negotiating table to end the war.[1] *They got it dead right.*

> We urge you to pair the military and economic support the United States has provided to Ukraine with a proactive diplomatic push, redoubling efforts to seek a realistic framework for a ceasefire.
>
> — thirty Congressional Democrats, in an open letter to Joe Biden

Had something changed fundamentally? Nope.

The letter was unvetted by the people that matter; within hours they were back-pedaling [2] and within a day they withdrew the letter as some sort of clerical mistake. Apparently, House Democrats and their friends in the military–industrial complex were unready or unwilling to end this war. [3] It was a monumental fuckup, both coming and going.

> The Congressional Progressive Caucus hereby withdraws its recent letter to the White House regarding Ukraine. The letter was drafted several months ago, but unfortunately was released by staff without vetting ... As Chair of the Caucus, I accept responsibility for this. Because of the timing, our message is being conflated by some as being equivalent to the recent statement by Republican Leader McCarthy threatening an end to aid to Ukraine if Republicans take over.
>
> — Progressive Democrats' retraction

> They couldn't even hold out for *24 hours*. What a complete humiliation. Joe Crowley must be sitting in his lobbyist office cackling each time this happens.
>
> — Glenn Greenwald, on the Democrats retracting their call for peace negotiations

The one person who seems to have a limited say is Zelensky. The chaos preceding the war, when the Ukrainians seemed confused by U.S./NATO rhetoric, presumably occurred during a period in which Zelensky and Putin were having discussions. It is said that Putin and Zelensky were working out a deal in April, when Boris Johnson showed up to let Zelensky know that no such deal would be tolerated.[4] NATO wanted its war, and no NATO puppet was gonna muck that up.

> Ukraine and Russia have largely resolved their differences, but the Biden admin is in the way.
>
> — William Arkin, *Newsweek*, April 2022

> Russia is open to negotiations over Ukraine, but any agreement with Kyiv would have little credibility because it could be rescinded by the West. This means that any possible settlement should be primarily discussed with the U.S.
>
> — Dmitry Peskov, Kremlin press secretary

Opinions   Editorial Board   The Opinions Essay

Opinions

In the long run, wars make us safer and richer

Zelensky's claim that they would "fight to the last Ukrainian" was boilerplate rhetoric to generate Western support. However, Ukraine passed a referendum stating that it would not negotiate with Putin: "we [Ukraine] are ready for dialogue with Russia, but with another president of Russia."[5] You *never* shut down communication channels. He was daring Vlad to kill every last Ukrainian. I'm not sure the Ukrainian soccer moms would sign off on that, but Vlad might.

> I would never want Ukraine to be a piece on the map, on the chessboard of big global players, so that someone could toss us around, use us as cover, as part of some bargain.
>
> — Volodymyr Zelensky, too late

The best thing we can do if we want the Russians to let us be Americans is to let the Russians be Russian.

— George F. Kennan

LINK TO REFERENCES

There are over 900 superscript references in the preceding pages. Each of them is a link to an online resource of some sort: an essay, a published article, a video, a Twitter post, etc.

For ease of access by readers of the paper version of this book, every one of those references can be found (and clicked on) at:

www.321gold.com/2022YIR/index.html

Made in the USA
Columbia, SC
15 March 2023

75056167-3b67-4719-af40-4199a993dd14R02